RIGHTS

VS.

PRIVILEGES

———

An analysis of two powerful privileged
interests that have deprived us of
fundamental rights

ROBERT DE FREMERY

———

*One can have a privilege only by depriving other men of
a portion of their rights. Consequently a reign of justice
will consist in the destruction of every privilege and the
restitution of every right.*

—Patrick Dove, 1850

PROVOCATIVE PRESS
SAN ANSELMO, CALIFORNIA 94960

Book design and production by Janet Andrews
Desktop Studio, San Anselmo, CA

Library of Congress Catalog Card No.: 92-64217
ISBN 0-96333820-0-4
Printed in the United States of America

To those who share my belief that we are capable of achieving a far more just society than what we have achieved so far and who are willing to keep working toward that goal.

The rights of men in society are neither divisible nor transferable nor annihilable, but are descendable only; and it is not in the power of any generation to intercept finally and cut off the descent. If the present generation, or any other, are disposed to be slaves, it does not lessen the right of the succeeding generation to be free; wrongs cannot have a legal descent.

—Thomas Paine

Do not imagine that the Parliaments and Courts of oppressors will ever right the wrongs of the oppressed. They exist for no such purpose ... Take the redress of your own wrongs into your own hands, as you are abundantly able to do, if you are only united, determined, and have clear ideas of your rights, and of what is needed to secure them.

—Lysander Spooner

INTRODUCTION

At the root of America's worst problems is the fact that we have never been true to Jefferson's principle: "Equal rights for all; special privileges to none."

When you allow special privileges to some, the rest of the population is put at a disadvantage which is magnified with each succeeding generation. Our economy collapses periodically, wealth becomes more and more concentrated in the hands of a few, and our taxes become more burdensome. Increasing poverty and continuous unemployment result in a mixture of despair and rage that leads to drug use and violent crime. And when conditions get bad enough, the likelihood of a military or Fascist coup increases.

Few Americans are aware of how close we came to the establishment of an authoritarian state during the depths of the Great Depression. In 1934 a Fascist coup was actually planned in this country. It was abandoned when General Smedley Butler refused to act as "leader" and published his report of the plot. A congressional committee investigated the incident, confirmed the existence of such a plot, and then proceeded to 'whitewash' the whole affair! The press said very little about it. Some papers even tried to laugh it off. *But that was not something to laugh about either then or today.*

Our country has once again become ripe for such an ugly happening because of our failure to correct the root causes of our problems. We were very lucky in 1934. We may not be so lucky next time.

I urge you, therefore, to read what follows carefully and thoughtfully. What this troubled world needs more than anything else is the example of just one country that has actually made a living reality of the Jeffersonian principle: Equal rights for all; special privileges to none. Then—*but not until then*—will it be possible to make genuine progress toward a peaceful world.

TABLE OF CONTENTS

A Chance Encounter

We met at Barth's Retreat—high up on Mt. Tamalpais just north of San Francisco. He was a retired doctor, a surgeon; I, a retired businessman. When he heard I was continuing with research in my lifelong interest in economics and politics he wanted to know where I stood. Was I a liberal, or a conservative, or what? The conversation proceeded as follows:

"I really don't know how to answer that. I suppose the most appropriate way to describe my views would be to call them radical."

"Radical?" He was clearly disturbed by the term.

"Yes, in the best sense of the word: going to the root of the problem. You doctors never hesitate to do that. If a leg has to be amputated in order to save a life, you don't hesitate to say so. Right?"

"What do you think the root of our problem is?"

"We never did enforce Jefferson's principle: Equal rights for all; special privileges to none. You believe in that principle, don't you?"

"Of course."

"Would it surprise you to know that two powerful interests other than slaveholders heavily influenced the writing of our Constitution and are still with us today—more powerful than ever?"

1

"It certainly would. What evidence is there of that?"

"James Madison's extensive notes taken at the Constitutional Convention. I take it you haven't read them?"

"No."

"You should. And read them carefully. Madison left no doubt about the influence of these privileged interests."

"Like what? Name them."

"Landholders and bankers."

"You sure sound like a radical all right. Don't you believe in free enterprise?"

"Absolutely. Far more than most people do."

"It sure doesn't sound like it."

"I'm not being inconsistent. We need landholders and bankers. But they should not have the special privileges our government gave them. Those privileges have prevented our free enterprise system from functioning properly. Unemployment, inflation, credit crunches, and the increasing concentration of wealth in the hands of a few are all traceable to those privileges."

"They are?"

"Yes. Tell me, do you think you have as much right to live in this country as anyone else?"

"Of course. Why do you ask?"

"You'll see in a minute. How do you explain the fact that some people have to pay others who may not even be citizens of this country for the right to be here?"

"What do you mean?"

"A person who owns no land at all has to live somewhere. So he is obliged to pay someone for the right to use, or occupy, part of this country. Isn't that so?"

"Yes. I see nothing wrong in that."

"But if we all have the same right to be here, then shouldn't any rent paid for the use of part of this country rightfully belong to all of us—share and share alike? How else can we assure the equal right of every citizen to be here?"

"I don't follow your reasoning."

"Suppose you are the sole owner of this whole country and all the rest of us had to pay you rent for whatever land we were using. Would it not be obvious that our rights to be here were inferior to yours, and that you were in a privileged position as compared with us?"

"Of course, especially if I were allowed to keep all the rent. I'd be fabulously wealthy without having to do a lick of work."

"*Allowed* to keep the rent? If you owned the whole country, it's a safe bet you would control the government and most of the legislation. I presume you would see to it that the laws allowed you to keep most of the rent."

"I suppose you're right about that. But what's this got to do with the situation in this country? You know as well as I that one man doesn't own it all."

"Suppose two men owned it all ... or 100 men ... or 1,000 men ... or anything less than all of us?"

"Now I see what you're getting at. You're saying that if each of us has an equal right to be in this country, then each has an equal right to the country, and therefore an equal right to its rental value. Is that it?"

"Exactly. Our land is our common heritage. It was here long before people existed. If any part of the rental value of our country—the land only—is privately pocketed, our common rights are being violated and privilege exists. But

3

don't get me wrong. I heartily approve of granting individuals exclusive use of part of our common heritage so long as each pays into a common fund the annual rental value of his or her privilege. How else can we be true to Jefferson's principle?"

"I don't know. Frankly I never looked at it this way before."

"Perhaps you should. Now let's carry this a little further. The total ground rent of this country naturally increases as our population increases. The rental value of land in the center of cities increases enormously. That means we have a source of public revenue that automatically increases as needed."

"Are you suggesting that our government wouldn't have to have any other revenue if it would just collect the rental value of land from all landholders?"

"Yes. Not our present government. But the kind of government we ought to have ... much smaller than the existing government."

"What a fascinating idea."

"It's been around for a long time. William Penn suggested the same thing clear back in 1693. In 1775 Adam Smith gave very good reasons why ground rent is the best source of public revenue. In 1850 Herbert Spencer, while developing his famous 'Law of Equal Freedom', argued substantially as I did about the equal right to be in a country. And twenty-nine years later, Henry George rediscovered the idea for himself and wrote his famous book *Progress and Poverty*."

"Henry George? That name rings a bell. Wasn't he known as the 'Single Taxer'?"

"Yes. He wanted to abolish all taxes except the tax on land value."

"That's the fellow. I didn't realize so many other famous men had the same idea before him. At any rate, I thought George's proposal had been pretty thoroughly discredited. Wasn't he a socialist?"

"Certainly not. He believed in free enterprise. It's true, of course, he stressed the importance of the common ownership of land. But he also believed in private tenure—which is really all we have today."

"What do you mean by that?"

"If any landholder doesn't pay his taxes, the land reverts to the government. He is assured of his right to use that part of our common heritage only so long as his taxes are paid."

"So it really wouldn't be any different from what we have today?"

"That's right—except that George wanted landholders to pay—in taxes—the full rental value of their land so that taxes on our homes, income, sales, etc. can be done away with. Such a shift of taxes—off Labor and Capital and their products, and onto Land—would assure a more equitable distribution of wealth."

"Would a landholder still be able to sell his land or bequeath it to his children as he can today?"

"Certainly. It would still be the same. And as long as the taxes are paid, the right to private tenure would be protected by the government. But of still greater importance, it would then be unnecessary for the government to violate our right to keep what we earn. Income taxes, sales taxes, gasoline taxes, taxes on our homes, factories, machinery, etc., all violate our property rights."

"But doesn't a tax on land violate our property rights also?"

"No. Land is our common property—not private property. We have private tenure—but that's all. So when the government collects the rental value of land via taxation, it is merely recovering a value that rightfully belongs to all of us. That does not violate anyone's property right. And by so doing, it actually makes it possible to fully protect our property rights in the wealth we create."

"I follow your line of reasoning all right. But you certainly have a different way of looking at things."

"Don't you think it's a better way? Does it make sense for the government to violate our right to keep and enjoy the fruits of our efforts just because it failed to assure us our equal right to be in this country? Wouldn't it make more sense to *protect* both rights instead of *violating* both rights?"

"When you put it that way, yes. But if you're right about this, why was George's proposal so thoroughly discredited?"

"It wasn't. It has been maligned, misrepresented, and misunderstood, but never proven wrong. As a matter of fact, by 1907 there was so much interest in Henry George's proposal that it was discussed at the annual meeting of the American Economic Association and there was overwhelming agreement on the soundness of the principles on which George's proposal was based."

"Then why wasn't something done about it?"

"It's not all that easy to make a change of this sort. Some scholars have even said it is too late to do it ... too unsettling for society."

"You disagree?"

"Can it ever be too late to establish justice? Hasn't that been the goal of humanity for thousands of years? Sometimes it's very difficult to take the next step toward that goal. But, as Herbert Spencer once said of this reform: 'Equity sternly commands that it be done.' ... You still agree, don't you, that every citizen in our country should have the same right as every other citizen to be here?"

"Yes, but ..." He didn't seem to know what to say.

"And you realize now that because we permit landholders to pocket most of the ground rent, vast fortunes have fallen into the hands of a privileged few while the economy suffers from a host of burdensome taxes that deprive millions of people of what ought to belong to them."

"Everybody has always hated taxes. But I'm not sure I understand how this other system would work. How would we get from here to there?"

"First we need to modify the existing property tax so that it falls only on what economists call the 'site value' of land. No improvements would be taxed. Then increase the tax on land so it equals the rental value of each site—the land only. And while doing that we should abolish the taxes on all buildings, homes, incomes, sales, gasoline, and all other taxes. Those taxes are robbing us of what ought to belong to us."

"And you think that would provide enough revenue to support all levels of government?"

"As I said before it wouldn't support the kind of government we have now—that's for sure! But we wouldn't need such a big government if our economy were functioning smoothly—as it soon would be if we had a sound tax system and a sound banking system. There would always be plenty of jobs for everybody at good wages. Our distribution of income would no longer be so unfair. We would no longer have the poverty and slums, drug use and violent crime, homeless and needy, that plague our large cities today. By going to the root of our problems the costs of local, state, and federal governments would decrease enormously."

"But suppose there were not enough revenue?"

"All right ... suppose there wasn't. Would that be any excuse for not using all the ground rent before resorting to other kinds of taxes? Isn't it important to try to establish equal rights for all—special privileges for none?"

"Yes, you've got me there." Another long pause. "What about all those who own no land? Wouldn't it be unfair for them to pay no taxes at all?"

"They will still be paying the full ground rent of the land to their landlords just as they are today. They can't escape that. That's what makes the present system so unfair. Today, all those who pay rent also pay a host of direct and indirect taxes in addition to the ground rent they have to pay their landlords. That's double taxation with a vengeance! The government has robbed them to such an extent that many require charity or public welfare to survive. From the standpoint of fairness, nothing could be more unfair than the present system. Also nothing could be more fair than the proposed system because every citizen would be contributing equally toward the cost of government."

"How do you figure that?"

"The rental value of this country rightfully belongs to

all of us—share and share alike. After collecting that value from each landholder, we could have the government distribute it equally to all of us. If, instead of that, we all agree to leave our equal shares with the government so that no other taxes need be levied, then we'll each be contributing the same amount toward the cost of government. Right?"

"Sounds logical. But I'm not so sure I like the idea of everyone contributing the same amount toward the cost of government."

"Why not?"

"It seems to me that those who make more should pay more. They can certainly afford it."

"That is true in some cases in our present system in which privileged interests can get huge incomes without doing a lick of work. But if we eliminate privilege ... as we should in order to establish equal rights for all ... differences in income would merely reflect differences in the contribution each of us makes toward society. For example, suppose there are two equally-skilled surgeons working at the same hospital but one puts in an eight-hour day whereas the other prefers to work only five hours a day so he can have more leisure time to do as he pleases. Would it be fair to make the doctor who worked the hardest pay more toward the cost of government? Wouldn't that discourage him from working so hard? And wouldn't society be the loser if he cut back on his workday because of being "fined", so to speak, for working harder?"

"O.K. You have made your point." He was quiet for a minute. "What about home-owners? Wouldn't this tax reform be pretty rough on them?"

"Why?"

9

"Wouldn't their land be taxed so heavily they'd lose their homes?"

"No. You're forgetting that homeowners would no longer be paying any taxes on their homes ... no more income taxes, no sales taxes, etc. Also the government would not be allowed to tax any piece of land more than the market indicates is fair. And every landholder would have the right of appeal just as he does under today's property tax."

"Isn't it difficult for an assessor to distinguish between the value of the land and the value of improvements?"

"They are already doing it. But I'll admit some of them do a very poor job. The point is that no matter how difficult it may be to distinguish between values that rightfully belong to the individual and values that should belong to society, we must make the effort to do so. It makes absolutely no sense to throw up our hands and let the government deliberately levy taxes on both kinds of value. Our homes shouldn't be taxed at all. And there shouldn't be any income tax nor sales tax. Such taxes violate our property rights. They also inhibit productive activity by depriving us of the fruits of our efforts. A tax on the rental value of land, however, doesn't violate anyone's property right. It is merely a payment for the privilege of exclusive use of part of our common heritage ... thus protecting everybodys' rights. And such a tax—unlike all others—actually encourages rather than discourages productive activity."

"Why is that?"

"It forces land speculators and investors to either improve their property or sell it to someone who will. There's no disagreement among economists on that."

"Wouldn't that lead to over-development?"

"Not at all. We want run-down housing and slums improved, don't we?"

"Of course. But I'm thinking of the need for parks, open spaces, and wilderness areas."

"This tax reform will make it much easier to have them."

"How so?"

"The price of land will fall. So it will be easier for us to acquire what we want for a park. Today we have to pay higher and higher prices to land speculators if we wish to buy their land for a park or open spaces. In a sound system, all we need to do is pay for any improvements on the property. The price of the land would be very little, if any … assuming of course, the assessor has been doing a good job. Government will lose income from that land, of course, because it will no longer be on the tax rolls."

"Seems to me you're being inconsistent."

"How so?"

"Earlier, you claimed there would be plenty of revenue to support all levels of government if this tax reform were made. Now you say that revenue would go down as newly-created parks come off the tax rolls."

"That decrease would be more than offset by an increase in revenue from all land remaining on the tax roll."

"How so?"

"By creating parks where needed, we make our country a more desirable place in which to live. We gladly pay more in order to live near parks and open spaces."

He was quiet for a minute. Then, "What about those who invested in real estate as a hedge against inflation?

11

Seems to me it would be unfair to them if this reform were to cause the price of land to fall."

"You're forgetting that the owner of improved real estate will no longer be paying taxes on the improvements. Remember?"

"But suppose it's unimproved land? Surely it wouldn't be fair for them to have to pay heavier taxes."

"How else can we establish each citizen's equal right to be here?"

"I don't know."

"Don't get me wrong. I recognize that land has been one of the best hedges against inflation. My wife and I have bought land solely for that reason. But we recognize that although it helps to protect *us*, it is not good for the rest of the community."

"Why not?"

"That land is being withheld from use. It's badly needed by builders. But we intend to continue holding it idle because we know the population pressure in that area will cause it to become more and more valuable as the years go by. We know of no better way to protect the value of our savings in these inflationary times. But when many people in our position are all doing the same thing, the result is an enormous quantity of good land being held idle while the price goes so high that builders finally get priced out of the market. That is not good for the economy."

"Is that the main cause of inflation and depression?"

"Some people think so. I don't. There is no question that the present tax system adds to inflationary pressures and aggravates our so-called business cycle. But inflation itself is caused by our unsound banking system. In other words, if we reformed our tax system and kept our unsound banking system, we'd still have the problem of inflation and unemployment even though less severe than before. The tax system, as I see it, is the main cause of our very inequitable distribution of wealth, whereas the banking system is the main cause of inflation and depression. ... But let's stick to the tax system for the present. Won't you agree it needs changing?"

"I can see it's a bad system all right. But I'm not sure of all the consequences of changing it. What about you and your wife and the land you've bought? If the full rental value of that land is recovered by the government, the price of your land would go way down, wouldn't it?"

"Yes."

"So you'd be worse off, wouldn't you? And wouldn't a drastic fall in the price of land hurt the economy?"

"Quite to the contrary—it would help the economy enormously. There are thousands of builders looking for lower-priced land so they can build homes at prices the public can afford to pay. And there are millions of persons who would like to have jobs and homes of their own. This tax shift will provide them with jobs and the purchasing power to buy homes. The entire economy would benefit."

"But what about you and your wife—and other investors like you. You would all lose the value of your investments in land. Right?"

"Yes ... but in most cases that loss would be more than offset by the elimination of all the other taxes we've been paying."

"But you would have destroyed your best hedge against inflation."

"True enough. That's why we must have banking reform also. As a matter of fact I doubt it would ever be politically feasible to put in the tax reform we need until inflation has been stopped and our banks put on a sound basis. And that won't happen without banking reform."

"With or without banking reform, the fact remains that investments in land would be wiped out. Won't that lead to demands for compensation?"

"I've already pointed out that most landholders—especially those with improved property—will be adequately compensated by the elimination of all the other taxes they have been paying. As for the others, does the government compensate those who invest in stocks and bonds when their prices fall? Of course not. So why should it compensate the land speculator?"

"I still don't like the idea of the government deliberately confiscating that one type of investment."

"Why not? If the rental value of land ought to belong to all of us, and if the values created by each individual ought to belong to the individual, then doesn't it make sense to have landholders return to the community what belongs to all of us so that the community can stop levying taxes on that which ought to belong to each of us?"

"But you will admit, won't you, that a few people may be hit pretty hard by a change of this sort?"

"Undoubtedly. But there's no question that an overwhelming majority would benefit."

"That bothers me. I've always believed our Constitution was set up to protect the rights of a minority."

"You're absolutely correct. The question is: *What are our rights*? Do we or don't we have an equal right to be here?

Should some of us have a greater right to be here than others? Shouldn't each person have the same right to enjoy the fruits of his or her productive activities without being taxed? Should any person have the right to pocket the rental value of land—our common heritage? Isn't it about time we made a living reality of Jefferson's principle: Equal rights for all; special privileges for none?"

"But I still feel an injustice would be done to some people who had invested in land."

"Look ... was an injustice done to the slave-holders when the slaves were freed?"

"No."

"Then what's your problem? The slaveholders had paid for their slaves ... and landholders have paid for their land. Justice required that the slaves be freed. And justice requires that every person in this country be granted his equal right to be here. Doesn't the same basic principle apply in both cases?"

"Yes, but wouldn't it at least be wise to make a change like this gradually ... say over a five or ten-year period instead of all at once?"

"Slavery wasn't abolished that way. I find it difficult to believe that when a great majority of the voters finally understand what their rights are, they will be content to take five or ten years to secure those rights. When people finally realize that the income tax, the sales tax, and taxes on their homes, etc. are violations of their property rights, I doubt they will be willing to wait ten years to have such legalized robbery stopped completely. Can you imagine our forefathers telling King George that our Declaration of Independence—which spelled out our rights as conceived at that time—was to be fully applicable five or ten years hence? ... that England's exploitation of us was to be eliminated gradually over ten years? I can't."

"But wouldn't you at least favor some sort of government aid for the few who would be hurt by the change?"

"That depends. There may be some who can no longer work and whose sole source of income has been from ground rent. And although they would have no legal claim against society, I do think they should be cared for adequately. It will certainly be much easier for us to help those few than it is for us to continue trying to care for the increasing millions of citizens who are driven into poverty by our present tax system."

"I still think there must be something wrong with all this."

"What makes you so doubtful?"

"I guess the main reason is that I keep thinking something would have been done sooner if it had been practical."

"The reason it hasn't been practical so far is that it hasn't been politically feasible. And it won't be politically feasible until more people understand the nature of rights and privileges. These things take time. Have you any idea how long it was before the Copernican theory was accepted?"

"No."

"About one hundred years after Copernicus died. Henry George died in 1897. He was the first one to really make a push for tax reform."

"But why should these things take so long?"

"A combination of factors. Perhaps the two most important are a confused public, and powerful privileged interests. The very questions you have raised are proof of the confusion that exists. I assure you that if you will take the time to explore this in depth ... consider it from all angles ... you will come to the conclusion, as others have, that the idea is sound. And never forget the basic issue—the Jeffersonian principle of equal rights for all and special privileges for none. There are moral questions involved here that simply cannot be ignored much longer. Many of our problems have arisen because we have not been true to Jefferson's principle. We simply cannot violate such a basic principle without suffering the consequences. We've already lost some of our rights, and we will most assuredly lose the rest of them unless we protect all of them. *Our rights are interdependent. They stand or fall together. Never forget that.*"

"I like your emphasis on rights."

"That's fundamental. That's what this country is all about ... or was intended to be anyway. But as yet not very many of our citizens understand what their basic rights are."

"Your emphasis on rights makes me think of the Libertarians. Yet I know they do not share your views about taxation."

"To a very large extent we do agree. Many of them say that *all* taxation is robbery. I say that all *except* a tax on ground rent is robbery. That certainly reflects far more agreement than disagreement."

"I can't argue with that." He was silent for quite awhile. "Now what about our bankers? Why did you call them privileged?"

"Because they are allowed to create most of what we use as money. And they get interest on the money they create.

Wouldn't you call that a powerful privilege?"

"Of course, if it's true."

"It is. Most of what we use as money consists of nothing but a lot of bookkeeping entries bankers create when they make loans. We draw checks against those bookkeeping entries."

"Are you saying that the checks we all use as money are not backed by real money ... hard cash?"

"That's exactly what I am saying. Bankers are not required to maintain 100% cash reserves behind their deposits that are withdrawable on demand. They are permitted to use most of those deposits for their own interest and profit. And they do. That's why we've had so many bank failures and panics throughout our history. And that's the root cause of the monetary and fiscal problems facing us today."

"Whew." He looked at his watch. "I sure wish I had more time to discuss all this with you further—but I've got to head for home. Have you written anything on these subjects?"

"Yes. I had several articles in the *Commercial and Financial Chronicle* of New York. The one about our tax system should clear up any doubts you may still have on that subject. The other articles dealt with our banking system. Each had to stand on its own, of course. But each contained important points that are not in the others. So I'll just send you excerpts from them."

"That's great. I'll be particularly interested in what you propose to do about the Federal Deposit Insurance Corporation and our banks. That situation has everybody worried."

"Of course it has. I'll also send you excerpts from a paper I submitted to the Federal Reserve Bank of San Francisco many years ago that has become more and more relevant as our banking troubles have increased. Had they paid attention to it when I first submitted it—and had we reformed our tax system along the lines we've been talking about—I am confident we wouldn't be in such a mess today."

"That's saying an awful lot."

"I realize that. But after you have read what I send you I think you will agree that we simply must make these changes."

He gave me his address, and departed.

Our Unsound Tax Laws and Measures for Reform

By Robert de Fremery
(Published in *The COMMERCIAL and FINANCIAL CHRONICLE*, July 7, 1960)

Daniel Webster once said: "A free government cannot long endure where the tendency of the laws is to concentrate the wealth of the country in the hands of a few, and to render the masses poor and dependent."

An objective analysis of our tax laws—as well as our banking laws—will, I believe, lead any fair-minded person to the conclusion that our laws do just that. They tend to concentrate wealth in the hands of a privileged few—taking from those who produce and giving to those who do not.

The basic defect in our tax system is that we allow our local, state, and Federal governments to tax away *privately created values* while at the same time an enormous amount of *publicly created value* remains in private hands.

Many are surprised to hear of publicly created value as distinct from privately created values. Victims of unjust taxation all their lives, they are shocked by the suggestion that it is possible to have an essentially burdenless tax system—that there is a natural reservoir of publicly created value, over and above all privately created values, which could pay for all legitimate activities of government. Yet many economists have recognized this fact for more than 200 years. And although we draw to some extent upon this source of revenue, the extent to which we do not is responsible for many of our economic ills today.

The difference between publicly created and privately created values, once seen, is never forgotten. Both result from the competitive bidding within society for the right to consume or use something. But it is of utmost significance that privately created values result from competitive bidding for goods and services produced by man, whereas publicly created values result from competitive bidding for something no man produced—the land upon which we live and work and whose value increases as the community in which it is located grows. In the one case men are bidding for goods and services produced by each other as private individuals. In the other men are bidding for the important right to use part of the earth's surface. In the one case you have privately created values. In the other you have a publicly created value.

Distinguishes Improvements from Land Rental Value

It is necessary, of course, to distinguish between the publicly created value of a piece of land and the value of improvements made by the landholder. A person may improve his land with his own money and effort by landscaping, planting crops, building a house or factory or other structure. Such improvements are privately created values. And when we speak of the publicly created value of a parcel of land, we are specifically excluding the value of any privately financed improvement in or on it.

22

As each community grows, both publicly created and privately created values grow with it. Privately created values increase as an expanding population produces more houses, more food, more manufactured products and more services. But this same activity together with the activities of local, state, and Federal governments causes an increase in the value of land over and above the total of all privately created values. For example, before Rockefeller Center could be erected, the bare land under it had to be leased from its owners. The rent agreed upon for this piece of bare land was $3 ½ million a year, a sum which is still being paid each year to its title-holders. Bare land in that location is worth that much to those who need to use it. Similar examples of the high rental value of land, apart from any improvements in or on it, can be found in every large city.

The increasing value of land resulting from the growth of each community is in no sense created by the productive effort of each title-holder. The land that is most favorably situated will have the highest value regardless of who holds title to it. Thus a man who contributes nothing to the community in which he lives—a man who produces nothing and performs no useful service to society—may, nevertheless, have a steadily increasing income because he holds title to a piece of land in the center of a growing city. The rental value of his land will steadily increase as the community grows. That is what is meant by a publicly created value. It is created by the community as a whole and exists independently of the productive activity of the landholder.

Stresses Basic Differences

The problems we have in taxation today result primarily

23

from our failure to take advantage of this basic difference between the publicly created value of land and privately created values of goods and services. We quite foolishly allow taxes to fall indiscriminately on both publicly created and privately created values. Privately created values should be sacredly protected as private property free of all taxes so as to encourage the maximum production of wealth. On the other hand the publicly created rental value of land—which no individual can rightfully claim as his alone because the public as a whole created it—should be looked upon as legitimate public property that, ideally, ought to be recovered by the community through taxation and used for public purposes. To the extent this is done a just revenue is derived that makes it unnecessary to levy taxes on privately created values.

Years of experience by assessors throughout the United States and in many other parts of the world have demonstrated that the publicly created value of land is readily separable from the value of private property in improvements. But if, in some cases, it is difficult to distinguish between publicly created and privately created values—between what is rightfully public property and what is rightfully private property—it is still inexcusable not to make the effort to do so. We cannot make secure to the individual what belongs to him until we make secure to the public what belongs to us. We cannot preserve a system of private property unless we make all levels of government draw revenue solely from what is legitimately public property.

Depicts Disadvantages of Present Tax System

Consider the disastrous consequences of not securing

public revenue from the proper source:

1. By failing to make full use of the publicly created value of land for public purposes, we have forced local, state, and Federal governments to obtain more and more revenue from privately created values. That means sales taxes, income taxes, taxes on our homes, factories, machinery, cigarettes, gasoline, and all the other sources from which governments try to raise revenue today. Such taxes discourage the production of wealth and add to inflationary forces by increasing costs of production.

2. By allowing a large part of the publicly created rental value of land to be privately pocketed, we encourage speculation in land. Vast amounts of excellent land in both city and country lie either under-developed or completely idle, the taxes being too low to induce the holders to put it to better use or sell it to those who will. The enormously inflated prices of land today are due to this cause and stand as a major roadblock to the construction industry. Thus, the June, 1958 issue of *House & Home* (leading magazine for the construction industry) editorialized as follows: "It just plain is not true that land for home building is getting scarce. What is true is that land speculators are making land scarce by holding millions of acres off the market to get higher prices (or pricing those acres out of today's market, which is the same thing in different words) ...

   "The one best way to stop land price inflation and perhaps squeeze out some of the past inflation is to get together and fight to put more of the tax load on land and less of the tax load on improvements. This shift might make it too costly for speculators to hold good home sites idle hoping to squeeze us for still higher prices later on.

"Higher taxes on land would hurt no one but the land speculators. Higher taxes on land would permit lower taxes on houses and other improvements. Higher taxes on land are the only taxes that would stimulate production instead of discouraging it.

"Our industry has to live closer to the land speculator than any other industry. We have a closer view of the harm land speculation is doing our economy, so we should be first to tell the tax planners and the tax collectors that higher land taxes are the one way to raise more revenue without hurting anyone except our public enemy No. 1."

Of course, the real culprit—our real public enemy—is not the land speculator but rather a tax system that encourages speculation in land. The public as a whole is responsible for its own misfortune by not insisting that the publicly created value of land be used as the source of public revenue.

3. When we deprive our citizens of the full reward for their productive activities by levying taxes on the things they buy, the homes they build, and the money they earn, a growing number of them will be unable to afford decent housing. Slums are an inevitable result. By taking taxes off income, sales, and houses and putting them on the publicly created value of land, lower income groups will be more able to afford decent housing, and slumlords will be

obliged to erect decent housing in order to pay their taxes.

4. When governments have the power—as they do today—to tax privately created values and spend the money on public improvements that add value to nearby land, it is inevitable that powerful lobbies representing these landholders will exert pressure to pass pork barrel legislation. On the state and Federal levels these lobbies strive to increase government spending for highways, dams, schools, etc., because no state or Federal revenue comes from taxes on land. Locally these lobbies are engaged in holding down property taxes which fall on their lands while boosting sales taxes and any other taxes that will substitute for taxes on their land-holdings. The result is an inherent tendency for the state and Federal governments to spend themselves into bankruptcy while local governments claim they are impoverished.

5. The combination of the above factors results in a natural tendency toward a loss of local responsibility and a growing dependence of local governments on central government—a trend that threatens the survival of free institutions as our forefathers knew them.

Criticizes Education System That Ignores Henry George

The peculiar nature of land value and its suitability as a source of public revenue has been recognized by many economists during the past 200 years. Adam Smith distinguished between ground rent and ordinary rent for the use of improvements. He said ground rent was a superior source of public revenue because taxes obtained from this source had no harmful effect on enterprise. John Stuart Mill referred to the rising growth of a community as an "unearned increment" if allowed to remain in the hands of landholders.

During the last half of the 19th Century, several scholars—each independently of the others—discovered this natural source of government revenue—this fund of publicly created value that makes it possible to have a burdenless tax system. But the man who did more than any other before him to clarify the distinctive nature of land value, and who thereby incurred the wrath of powerful landholding interests, was the United States economist and social philosopher, Henry George. No man in the last 100 years has received more abuse and been so grossly misrepresented. Yet he succeeded in winning the acclaim of statesmen, philosophers, economists, and leading citizens all over the world.

Henry George was a man of intense faith. He firmly believed in a moral order and in the beneficence of natural laws. He saw clearly that the value of land is the natural source of public revenue because not only is it a publicly created value over and above all privately created values *but it grows as the need for public revenue grows.* And he realized the awful truth that because the value of land grows as each community grows, a blight will fall on any community in direct proportion to its refusal to obey natural law by obtaining its revenue from this source. He saw that to the extent publicly created values are privately pocketed, a relatively few landholders become wealthy while the vast majority of people are kept relatively poor under a crushing burden of direct and indirect taxes on their productive activity. He saw that if a government robs the people of the fruit of their efforts while at the same time giving a favored few values to which they are not entitled, the moral fibre of both groups will be destroyed. The basic principles so ably espoused by Henry George have been endorsed by Leo Tolstoy, Woodrow Wilson, David Lloyd George, Henry Ford, John Dewey, Albert Einstein, Winston Churchill, Theodore Roosevelt, Albert Jay Nock, Rabbi Stephen S. Wise, Sun Yat Sen, Louis D. Brandeis, Clarence Darrow, Irving Fisher, John R. Commons, Samuel Gompers, and many others. But the sad fact is that few high school or college graduates have heard either of him or of the clear and just principles he sought to popularize—*principles which have never been refuted.* Commenting on this neglect, Tolstoy said: "The chief weapon against the teaching of Henry George was that which is always used against irrefutable and self-evident truths. This method, which is still being applied in relation to George, was that of hushing up."

Economists' Views in 1907 and Currently

Largely as a result of Henry George's influence on economic thought, the American Economic Association had a roundtable discussion of land value taxation at its annual meeting in 1907. The final canvass of opinion showed that an overwhelming majority of those present agreed on the soundness of the following three propositions:

1. The site value of land is a creation of the community,

not a creation of the landholder.

2. A tax levied on the site value of land cannot be shifted nor recovered from the tenant by raising his rent.

3. A tax levied on the site value of land is burdenless. The community, in taxing site value, is merely recovering a value it has created.

That was over 50 years ago. Recently, Dr. Glenn E. Hoover, past President of the Pacific Coast Economic Association, observed that most economists today maintain the same position.

Many prominent statesmen during and after Henry George's life recognized the validity of his teaching. Notable among these were Winston Churchill and Theodore Roosevelt. Mr. Churchill gave two brilliant speeches attacking land monopoly—one in the House of Commons, the other in Edinburgh. In the Edinburgh speech, Churchill said: "I hope you will understand that, when I speak of the land monopolist, I am dealing more with the process than with the individual landowner. I have no wish to hold any class up to public disapprobation. I do not think that the man who makes money by unearned increment in land is morally a worse man than anyone else who gathers his profit where he finds it in this hard world under the law and according to common usage. It is not the individual I attack, it is the system. It is not the man who is bad, it is the law which is bad. It is not the man who is blameworthy for doing what the law allows and what other men do; it is the State which would be blameworthy were it not to endeavor to reform the law and correct the practice. We do not want to punish the landlord. We want to alter the law."

Churchill never retracted any of these statements. Quite to the contrary, they were verified and confirmed by inclusion in a volume, *Liberalism and the Social Problem*, which he later made public. In the preface to that work he wrote: "The opinions and arguments are unaltered and hereby confirmed, and I press them earnestly and insistently upon the public."

Taunted recently in the House of Commons with once having "sung the land song," he retorted, "I shall sing it again."

Theodore Roosevelt, in a speech delivered Aug. 6, 1912, showed his grasp of the subject: "Alaska should be developed at once, but in the interest of the actual settler. The government should keep the fee of all of the coal fields and allow them to be operated by lessees, with the condition in the lease that nonuse shall operate as a forfeit. Moreover, it would be well in Alaska to try a system of land taxation which will, so far as possible, remove all the burdens from those who actually use the land, whether for building or for agricultural purposes, and will operate against any man who holds the land for speculation or derives an income from it based, not on his own exertions, but on the increase in value due to activities not his own."

"Why," one may ask, "hasn't the world made better use of sound tax principles if economists and leading statesmen have recognized their validity?" Local governments in the United States—through the property tax—have made some use of land value as a source of revenue. But there has been a great change since World War I. The percentage of total public revenues coming from land has steadily declined since that time—partly because of the burdensomeness of

31

that part of the property tax that falls on improvements and personal property, and partly because of the enormous political influence of landed interests which always look to the state and Federal governments or to local nonproperty taxes for substitute funds that should be raised by local taxes on the rental value of land.

Countries That Are Taxing Land

Some areas of the world, notably Australia, New Zealand, and Denmark, have made good use of sound tax principles by perfecting the property tax. Instead of allowing this tax to fall on both land and improvements, they have removed, or are in the process of removing, all taxes on improvements and putting the full burden of this tax on land, where it belongs. The resulting stimulus to the construction industry is always apparent. Higher taxes on land induce land speculators to sell their idle holdings, thus making land available to builders. The removal of taxes from buildings obviously encourages construction.

But although these countries have made progress in the right direction by removing taxes on improvements, they still have a long way to go. There are still many taxes falling on privately created values while an enormous amount of publicly created land value remains in private hands. *The high price of bare land is proof of this fact.*

Progress in the direction of a completely sound revenue system will follow readily once the public thoroughly understands the subject. The reason the public doesn't understand taxation is that the basic principles have been woefully misrepresented by powerful privileged interests. For example, it is claimed these principles threaten our system of private property. Exactly the opposite is true. These principles assert an absolute, unqualified property right in all that a man's enterprise, ingenuity and exertion enable him to produce. If you build a house, or raise a herd of cattle, or work for a weekly pay check, it should be yours completely and absolutely. Your ownership should not be required to meet any conditions imposed by a tax collector. There should be no income tax, no corporation tax, no tax on buildings or machinery, no tax on trade, no sales tax. As Henry George put it: "Instead of weakening and confusing the idea of property, I would surround it with stronger sanctions. Instead of lessening the incentive to the production of wealth, I would surround it with stronger sanctions. Instead of lessening the incentive to the production of wealth, I would make it more powerful by making the reward more certain...No matter how many millions any man can get by methods which do not involve the robbery of others—they are his; let him have them."

Taxed Property Is Not Private Property

Another bogeyman is the question of who would own the land if all revenue came from land values. Here again some have become confused over the meaning of private property. To the extent that property is taxed, it ceases to be private. What a man creates or earns can be considered as truly private property only if it is his to do with as he sees fit—free of any taxes levied upon it. Private property must therefore be understood as *property that is not subject to taxation*. Since taxes should fall solely on publicly created land values, it is correct to say that land should not be classified as private property in that sense. But bear in mind we do not have this kind of private property in land today, nor do we have private property in anything! Taxes fall on our land, our homes, our incomes, our purchases, our inheritances. That's just what we should object to. Public revenue should come solely from the publicly created value of land. We should hold as private property, *tax free*, all privately created values. How else can we encourage the production of wealth? Let our land—which should be looked upon as our common heritage—continue to be privately held, but require each landholder to pay into the public treasury the publicly created rental value of the land he holds. Justice demands no less. Then, and then only, will it be possible to protect privately created values by freeing them of taxes.

Sees It Lessening Government Power

The question is sometimes asked: Doesn't land value taxation place too much power in the hands of government? No. It has the opposite effect. Modern governments are dangerous because we have given them the power to take privately created values away from us. When we allow our governments to deprive us of the fruits of our labors, we impair our ability to fend for ourselves. Many of us are forced to become wards of the state. The only effective way to limit the power of government and to make certain it remains our servant is to deny it the power to deprive a man of the fruit of his effort. We should compel all levels of government to live within their legitimate income, the publicly created value of land, the amount people are willing to pay for exclusive use of the land they hold. Governments are not entitled to more than this. And it is particularly wrong for any government to deprive any citizen of privately created values—which is now being done on a grand scale—as long as a single dollar of publicly created value remains in private hands.

Curiously enough, the reverse of the above question is sometimes used as an argument against sound tax reform. It is claimed that the proposed system of taxation would weaken the government unduly and place it in the embarrassing position of being unable to make both ends meet. There are several answers to this. First, if our governments no longer took from us the values we create as individuals, we would no longer have to be taken care of by our government to the extent we are today. Second, when we secure public revenue from the proper source, we have less "pork barrel" legislation. Landholders become watchdogs of the public purse rather than pressure groups asking for more spending for highways, dams, and irrigation projects that will increase the value of their landholdings without their having to pay for it. Third, when taxes are removed from improvements or other privately created values, the demand for land naturally increases. People will pay more for the exclusive use of land which they can improve without being taxed for the improvement. Thus the public revenue from land values rises as other taxes are removed.

It may still be argued, however, that our various levels of government may want more income than they can get from the annual rental value of land. Maybe they will. But that is no excuse for allowing them to leave a large part of their legitimate revenue in private hands today. If, after our tax system is put on a sound basis, our governments still do not have sufficient revenue to make both ends meet, then there is reason to believe we should cut down the size of our government. We must resist the attempt of governments to confiscate privately created values. There is no other way to respect the right to private property—the foundation of our free enterprise system.

Claims Landowner Would Be Freer Than He Is Today

Another common misunderstanding is that somehow a thorough going system of land value taxation would mean that the government rather than private individuals would have the power to allocate sites as a consequence of which we would all be subservient to the government. But that is not the case. It would still be up to the market place to determine the use to which land is put. There would still be a free market in land. Titles to land would still be exchanged—but at greatly reduced prices. Each landholder would be just as free as he is today to put his land to its best use. As a matter of fact, he would be much more free than he is today because the amount of taxes he pays will be independent of the improvements he puts on his land. He will no longer be taxed for improving his land.

Some landholders misjudge the effect of tax reform. They don't realize how much they stand to gain from a sound tax system. The higher taxes we would pay on the land we hold would be more than offset by the elimination of taxes on improvements and personal property, of income and sales taxes, and the huge burden of indirect taxes hidden in the price of goods and services purchased. The only sufferers from this reform will be the relatively few speculators in underdeveloped land or those whose income is derived primarily from ground rent rather than from the rendering of a useful service to society. Surely it should not be difficult for those who wish to preserve our free enterprise system to decide whether or not we should continue protecting the special interests of this small segment of the population at the expense of everyone who is engaged in useful productive activity. Surely we have the wisdom to stop this senseless taxation of privately created values when there is an ample supply of publicly created value that can be used to support our local, state, and Federal governments.

Another stumbling block that prevents some people from accepting sound tax reform is their belief that if taxes on the value of land are increased, a landholder who has invested in land so as to have the privilege of pocketing funds obtained by leasing the land to others should be compensated by the government when he loses this privilege. But why should anybody be compensated just because the government changes its source of revenue? Was anybody compensated when the income tax was put into effect? Of course not. The whole idea of compensation is absurd. All taxation, no matter where it falls, involves the confiscation of value. No matter where the government gets its revenue, confiscation of value takes place. The government takes values that are privately held and puts them to use for public purposes. It is absurd, therefore, to compensate the landholder just because taxes on the publicly created value of his land are increased. As a matter of fact, if anybody deserves compensation, it is all those who have been robbed of their privately created values under the existing tax system, not those who have been permitted to pocket the publicly created value of land all these years. But if we are wise, we will not try to correct past injustices. We will simply insist that justice be done from now on.

Finds Single Tax to Be Most Equitable

Another variation of the above argument is the claim that it would be wrong to obtain all public revenue from landholders when a large number of citizens have no land. But those who have no land are paying ground rent to those who do. In other words landless people provide landholders with the money to pay taxes falling on their land. And if we bear in mind the essential difference between publicly created and privately created values, we are forced to the conclusion that taxes on the publicly created rental value of land are the only taxes that are absolutely equitable to all citizens. This is so because the annual rental value of land, being a publicly created value, legitimately belongs to all, share and share alike. Theoretically, our government should recover the total rental value of land—our common heritage—and divide it equally among all citizens. But since our governments need revenue and we wish to avoid having taxes levied on privately created values, it makes sense for each citizen to assign to his local government his equal share of this public value. By so doing he contributes the same as every other citizen to the cost of government. Certainly there is no other source of revenue as equitable as this.

Denies Tax Can Be Shifted

At the opposite extreme of the claim that land value taxation is wrong because landholders would be the only ones paying taxes is the claim that landholders would be paying no taxes at all. It is claimed that they would merely raise their rents in proportion to the increase in taxes falling on their lands. But this is one thing all reputable economists agree can not be done. If site A (land only) in the heart of a city is worth $1,000 per month to whoever uses it, while site B (land only) on the outskirts of the city is worth only $100.00 per month, then site A is worth only $900.00 more per month than is site B. A change in the amount of taxes falling on these two landholders cannot affect the relative value of these sites. Suppose, for example, that an attempt were made to get $2,000 and $200.0 per month respectively for these two sites just because each landholder were required to pay taxes of $1,000 and $100.00 respectively to the city. Obviously, the tenants in site A would move to lower cost land. Site A is not worth $1',800 more per month than site B. If it were, the landholder would be getting it in today's market. Although a tax on land values affects the price of land, it cannot affect its rental value. There is no disagreement among economists on this point.

Explains Mechanics of Tax Collection

The question naturally arises: How should Federal, state, and local governments obtain the rental value of land? The practical answer is that we should return to the constitutional provision that requires our Federal government to apportion direct land taxes among the states according to their respective populations. The states, in turn should obtain this revenue and the revenue for their own support by apportionment among their counties, in the way Nebraska, Texas, Montana, and a number of other states still do. The counties, as agents of the states, should collect their

39

revenue, and the revenue needed by state and Federal governments, from the rental value of their lands, using existing property tax collection machinery. These changes would reverse the trend of the last 50 years. Instead of lower levels of government becoming increasingly dependent upon higher levels of government for aid, thereby losing their independence, the higher levels of government would return to dependence upon the lower. That is as it should be if we wish to preserve our liberties.

Some may claim, "It's too late to change the rules of the game." But if a person has a clear understanding of the disastrous effect that some of the existing rules are having upon us—he will realize the wisdom of making the rules sounder so as to protect each person's right to enjoy the fruits of his efforts. The first barrier to the spread of Communism is a tax system that differentiates between publicly created and privately created values. Then and only then can all privately created values be treated as private property, secure in private hands, immune from confiscation by tax collectors.

In his book, *Constructive Taxation for Free Enterprise*, Judge John R. Fuchs stated the issue clearly as follows: "There can be no hope of peace and order in society without a clear recognition of what is public and what is private property. The soundness of the very foundation of society depends upon this... We must distinguish between what is Mine, Thine, and Ours."

Almost two thousand years age, a famous teacher of Nazareth stated the same basic principle when he said: "Render unto Caesar that which is Caesar's." Truly there is nothing new under the sun. ... Our problems are the same.

We cannot escape the consequences of our immoral acts. We cannot hope to achieve the kind of life our Creator intended for us until we provide ourselves with a sound and just method of raising public revenue, and a sound monetary system.

The earth is given as a common stock for men to labor and live on ... Wherever in any country there are idle lands and unemployed poor, it is clear that the laws of property have been extended beyond human right.

—Thomas Jefferson

It is the value of the improvement only, and not the earth itself, that is individual property. Every proprietor, therefore, of cultivated lands, owes to the community a ground-rent (for I know of no better term to express the idea) for the land which he holds ...

—Thomas Paine

The country needs a new and sincere thought in politics, coherently, distinctly and boldly uttered by men who are sure of their ground. The power of men like Henry George seems to me to mean that.

—Woodrow Wilson

Land monopoly is not the only monopoly, but it is by far the greatest of monopolies—it is perpetual monopoly, and it is the mother of all other forms of monopoly. Unearned increments in land are not the only form of unearned or undeserved profit, but they are the prinicpal form of unearned increment, and they are derived from processes which are not merely not beneficial, but positively detrimental to the general public.

—Winston Churchill

The right of the landlord to appropriate the monopoly rent of the land is by no means absolute, being subject to the power both of eminent domain and of taxation. ...

Therefore, the rights of any man upon the earth must be reconciled with the equal rights of other man, not only of living men but of the unborn generations. ...

The true doctrine surely is that men hold property in limited and necessary natural resources, not as sovereigns, but as tenants—who have rights and also duties of mankind.

—Walter Lippmann

Henry George was one of the really great thinkers produced by our country ... I wish his writings were better known and more clearly understood.

—Franklin D. Roosevelt

Henry George is the only economist I ever read with whom I could find no fault.

—Dorothy Thompson

There's a sense in which all taxes are antagonistic to free enterprise—and yet we need taxes ... So the question is, which are the least bad taxes? In my opinion the least bad tax is the property tax on the unimproved value of land, the Henry George argument of many, many years ago.

—Milton Friedman

Property taxes could profitably be revised to fall more heavily on land, rather than, as at present, penalizing property improvements.

—Jack Kemp

BANKING AND MONETARY REFORMS
TO PRESERVE PRIVATE ENTERPRISE*

by Robert de Fremery
(Excerpts from the article published in The
COMMERCIAL and FINANCIAL CHRONICLE,
June 7, 1956)

An increasing number of articles and speeches have been devoted to the question of whether we should give the Federal Reserve Board standby controls over instalment credit. One need not look far to find the reason we are being asked to sanction these ever-increasing government controls. Wm. McChesney Martin, Chairman of the Federal Reserve Board, stated the reason very clearly as follows: "It should be borne in mind that expansion in commercial banking operations creates new supplies of money in contrast to other financial institutions which lend existing funds." (Testimony before Senate Banking Committee.)

In other words, we must distinguish between the lending of credit, i.e., "new supplies of money" and the lending of "existing funds." If all loans were made with existing

---

* Milton Friedman—after reading this article in full—wrote me as follows: "I thought it an extraordinarily effective piece, well calculated to persuade and inform." (letter, 7/5/56)

funds, there would be no valid reason for any government interference, regulation, or control of the lending of those funds. The lending of bona fide savings is merely the lending of a surplus. That is a civilized process that should be encouraged. It should not be controlled and regulated by the government. Nor should there be any fear over the volume of debt arising from such lending. It is desirable that all our resources—including bona fide savings—be put to maximum use.

Why then do we tolerate government interference in the money market? Why all these "credit controls?" Why all this concern over the volume of debt? Because—as Mr. Martin pointed out—when our commercial banking system expands its operations, it does so by lending "new supplies of money" (bank credit), rather than by lending existing funds.

The importance of this fact can not be over-emphasized. Our entire price structure today is in terms of bank credit originating from earlier expansions of commercial bank operations. Over 90% of what we are using as money is nothing but bank credit. And because our past experience with bank credit has shown that it is highly unstable, and that undue fluctuations in its supply can have disastrous effects upon our economic system, we have been forced to accept ever-increasing government controls of our banking system.

Need we fear these controls? Yes. No man or group of men should have the power to arbitrarily manipulate the supply of money or to determine the channels into which savings should flow. The power to change the supply of money is a tremendous power. It is the power to force debtors into slavery; it is the power to dispossess people of their property; it is the power to rob people of the value of their savings. And the power to determine the channels into which savings should flow is the power to control the entire economic system. The existence of such powers is totally incompatible with the survival of freedom—both economic and political. And yet, under the existing banking system, if we do not grant these powers to the Federal Reserve Board, a semi-public agency, then they will remain in the hands of our commercial banks and market forces which in the past produced such violent fluctuations in the supply of money (bank credit) as to nearly destroy our free enterprise system.

Dilemma Confronting Us

That is the dilemma that confronts us. How can we preserve the monetary stability that is needed for the proper functioning of a free economic system without being forced into a financial dictatorship that is incompatible with the survival of our free economic system?

If we keep in mind the basic cause of our dilemma, we should have no trouble figuring a way out of it. If the basic justification for government controls of banking is that an expansion in commercial banking operations creates new supplies of money, why not convert commercial banks into institutions that can lend only existing funds? If this could be done without unduly upsetting our financial markets, and if some provisions can be made for additions to the supply of money as needed to serve an expanding population, then we could enjoy monetary stability without the threat of a financial dictatorship.

Why Change Banking?

There are many good reasons why we should seriously consider making such a change in our banking system. In the first place, this reform is the next logical step in the evolution of banking. Over 100 years ago—after the era of wildcat banking—it was recognized that banks should not have the power to issue their own notes. That power was taken away from the banks. What we failed to realize at that time was that the power to create deposits-subject-to-check is equivalent to the power to issue notes. So although one-half the weakness in our banking system was corrected, the other half remained—as has been amply demonstrated by the many bank panics suffered since that time.

Now that almost all students of the subject agree that there is no basic difference between notes and checks, we should complete the reform of our banking system by making it unlawful for banks to create deposits—taking care to first monetize the existing volume of bank credit (now being used as money) so as to prevent a severe deflation.

A second important reason for making such a change is that bank credit is a fundamentally dishonest type of money. The lending of bank credit is tantamount to the lending of an imaginary surplus. The bank deposits so created are fictitious. The banker—by lending his credit payable in money on demand—places himself in the position of promising to do something that is physically impossible to do. And the further bank credit is extended—the more precarious the position of the banker becomes—until finally confidence is lost and the whole flimsy structure of bank credit collapses.

Bank Credit Causes Inflation

A third important reason for making such a change is that the use of bank credit as a substitute for money is a most unsound procedure. The commonly accepted definition of money is that it is a medium of exchange and a standard of value. Bank credit—even though used as money—is merely a promise to pay money. This is a very important distinction that is too often overlooked. Bank credit is a shortsale of money. And like shortsales of anything else, shortsales of money upset the true value relationship between money and the goods and services to be exchanged for money. In other words, bank credit causes inflation. Prices are inflated whenever they are higher than they ought to be. And if our money is diluted with bank credit, then prices are higher than they ought to be. This concept of inflation is a little different from the orthodox conception of inflation—but it is far more meaningful. No understanding of the cause of deflations (depressions) is possible unless we have a correct understanding of what constitutes inflation.

There are those who believe that once bank credit has been allowed to expand, nothing can be done to prevent a collapse (that is, nothing economically sound and consistent with a free economic system). The Austrian school—best represented by the writings of Ludwig von Mises—takes this stand as evidenced in the following statement: "There is no means of avoiding the final collapse of a boom brought about by credit expansion. The alternative is only whether the crisis should come sooner as the result of a voluntary abandonment of further credit expansion, or later as a final and total catastrophe of the currency system involved." (*Human Action*, p. 570).

Dr. von Mises believes that the expansion of bank credit causes malinvestment and a squandering of scarce factors of production that will inevitably lead to a crash and ensuing depression. But a more plausible theory is that all economic activity is continually reaching a new equilibrium between the total circulating medium of exchange and the goods and services offered for it. In other words, an expansion of bank credit leads to a collapse not because of mis-directions in production but rather because of the operation of Gresham's Law. The use of bank credit as a medium of exchange gives us what Bishop Berkeley called a "double money." Even though bank credit is supposedly convertible into money on demand, nevertheless it is not as good as money. It is a short sale of money. And as the volume of these shortsales increases it is inevitable that Gresham's Law will eventually operate, i.e., the undervalued money (gold or legal tender 'fiat' money) will be exported or hoarded—thus causing a collapse of bank credit.

According to this theory, it is possible to avoid a collapse following a period of credit expansion simply by converting the existing volume of bank credit into actual money having an existence independent of debt, and at the same time take away the banking system's privilege of creating any more credit, i.e., force banks to confine their lending operations to the lending of existing funds.

...

Once having stabilized the banking system so that it could no longer be the source of changes in the supply of money, it would then be necessary to protect ourselves

50

from arbitrary manipulation of the supply of money by the government. That raises the question: What should determine changes in the supply of money?

How to Change Money Supply

Such well known economists as Bradford Smith (U. S. Steel Corp.), C. A. Phillips, F. A. Bradford, Carl Snyder, and James Angell, have suggested that the supply of money should vary directly as population, i.e., as our population increases, our supply of money should be increased proportionately. Then the supply and demand relationship between population and money will result in a dollar of constant value. Such a dollar would buy more physical goods as techniques of production improve and costs are therefore going down. But this would not be deflationary because prices would not fall faster than costs except in those industries suffering from a shift in consumer demand. And prices should fall faster than costs in such industries in order to facilitate a shift in the basic factors of production from "less wanted" forms of wealth into "more wanted" forms of wealth.

Such a dollar would also always do justice between debtors and creditors because it would always be equally difficult to obtain.

No Inflation or Deflation

Were we to adopt such a system at this time, we would remove the threat of inflation and deflation while at the same time removing the necessity for any government controls of the lending operations of banks. We could henceforth cease to worry about the amount of consumer debt. All savings should be loaned so as to keep money in circulation. Debts that arise from the lending of actual savings are perfectly sound so long as ordinary caution is used by the lender. It is debts that arise from the lending of credit that cause our price level to become inflated. And the threat of deflation that faces us today is due to the fact that our price level is in terms of bank credit rather than in terms of money having an existence independent of debt. By converting that bank credit into money, we will have removed the threat of deflation.

Perhaps the most important result of such a change would be that our bankers and our business men could now rely on the stability of the per capita supply of money. Neither our banking system nor our government would have the power to expand or contract the per capita supply of money. Keep in mind that no new purchasing power would be given to, nor would any be taken away from, any person who doesn't already have access to that purchasing power today. We would merely be putting actual money where people now think money is—merely converting credit (which is now being used as money) into money that has an actual existence.

Non-Collapsible Money Market

Bankers would now be free to make the savings of the country readily available for loans without the fear of a possible collapse of the money market. That's not true today. At present bankers are fully aware of the instability of bank credit. Therefore a conservative banker—anxious to protect his depositors as much as possible—is reluctant to lend credit on long term during a boom because his deposits are withdrawable on demand or at most on 30 days notice. And the government—also aware of how unstable the banking system is—has surrounded bankers with a mass of red tape, rules, and regulations in a vain effort to protect the public from this essentially unsound operation.

Under this new system, the bankers and the government would know that the money market had a solid, non-collapsible base. They would know that the basic cause of bank panics had been removed. The only restriction on banks would be that they would no longer have the right to create credit as they do now.

...

Some bankers will call the plan "inflationary" and some will call it "deflationary". But it should be clear that neither accusation is valid. No additional purchasing power would be added to the system—nor would any be taken out of the system. We would merely be stabilizing at the existing per capita supply of dollars. We would merely be converting bank credit—which is now being used as money—into actual money. This new money will be money that ought to be in the banks today—but isn't. It is money that belongs to those who have checking accounts. Checks are continually being drawn against those deposits. But at present those deposits have no existence except on the books of the banks. And because that situation prevails with all our banks, our price structure is not on a firm basis. By putting a 100% reserve behind all checking accounts we will be putting our price structure on a sound basis.

...

It might appear that if we stop using bank credit as money there will be a great reduction in the liquidity and transferability of wealth. That would be true if we did not monetize the existing volume of bank credit. Bank credit is nothing but a substitute for money—and a very poor substitute at that. One of the functions of money is to make wealth liquid and facilitate the transfer of wealth. The curse of using bank credit as money is that when bank credit collapses, the liquidity of wealth is destroyed. That's why we have depressions. If we furnish ourselves with an adequate supply of money—and stabilize that money by making credit banking illegal—we will then be assured of continuous liquidity.

Population vs. Gold Standard

The question arises: Would it be wise to have such a currency convertible into gold? Certainly not. That would make it credit currency—the very thing that has caused so much trouble. ... The stability of international trade depends primarily upon the stability of the currencies used in international trade. And by abandoning the use of credit as money—thereby stabilizing the dollar—we will be doing the most that can be expected of us toward the establishment of conditions that would make possible an expansion of world trade on a sound basis.*

There are some people who look with distrust upon "printing press" or "fiat" money. But they overlook one of the basic facts about money. It is true that we need a "hard" money. But we should not make the mistake of associating "hardness" with convertibility into gold. The essence of a

---

* An excellent book on this subject is *International Monetary Issues*, Charles R. Whittlesey, McGraw-Hill, 1937.

hard money is not determined by the material of which it is composed—or the material into which it is convertible. The essence of a hard money is that its supply is fairly stable and there are precise limits to it. In other words, gold itself is a comparatively hard money because the supply of gold is inelastic. Bank credit convertible into gold is a very soft money because it is elastic and there are no precise limits to its supply, i.e., it expands and contracts. And a purely paper or "fiat" money can be a hard money if we set precise limits to its supply, or it can be a soft money if we set no precise limits to its supply. A population standard, as described above, would obviously give us a much harder money than the orthodox gold-credit system gave us prior to 1933—and certainly a much harder currency than the money-managers are giving us today.

The time is ripe for a thorough study of the principles upon which our monetary system ought to operate. ... We must think solely in terms of sound economic principles.

It's a challenge—a very great challenge. If we face it, and solve the problem, we will be taking the first constructive step back toward sanity in national and international relations. If we fail to accept the challenge, we will continue sinking into the mire of collectivism—hopelessly weighted down by the ever-increasing problems arising from an economic system that can't regulate itself because it lacks a stable and reliable standard of value.

*Be it not a mighty Privilege for a Private person,
to be able to create an hundred Pounds with a
Dash of his Pen?*
—George Berkeley, *The Querist*, 1735

*All the perplexities, confusion and distress in
America arise ... from downright ignorance of the
nature of coin, credit and circulation.*
—John Adams, in a letter to
Thomas Jefferson, 1787

OUR UNSOUND MONETARY SYSTEM AND MEASURES FOR REFORM

By Robert de Fremery
(Excerpts from the article published in *The COMMERCIAL and FINANCIAL CHRONICLE*, November 20, 1958)

When Paul M. Millians, Vice-President of Commercial Credit Company, spoke before the 40th International Consumer Credit Conference in San Francisco on July 19, 1954, he made the following revealing statement: "Most of the 17 major depressions in American history have been money panics. ...They were marked by a scramble of bank depositors to withdraw funds; restricted deposits; restricted credit; forced liquidation of bank loans; and forced liquidation of commodities."

A very similar statement was made by J. W. Gilbart—one of the leading bankers in England during the last half of the 19th Century: "It has been remarked that panics recur at regular intervals of about ten years each; nor can this be wondered at, seeing that the years 1825, 1837, 1847, 1857, and 1866 have, from various causes, been marked by the catastrophes so named. Judging by this recurrence of disasters at an apparently fixed period, it is not surprising that in the popular mind there seems to be a belief that a cycle exists, fated to bring in its train ruin to the monetary world and to millions outside of it. The dominant causes of the panics of the years specified, and their distinguishing characters, differ in some essential particulars. In one feature, indeed, they are all alike—the unreasoning fear which heralds, accompanies, accelerates and sometimes produces them." (J. W. Gilbart, *The History, Principles, and Practice of Banking*, Vol. 2, p. 334.)

These two men stated indisputable facts that are known to all who have a knowledge of business cycle theory. It is only the *interpretation* of those facts that leads to controversy among economists. One group claims that our banking system is basically sound and that panics are either due to causes originating outside the system or to abuses of that system. The other group claims that there is an inherent defect in our banking system that makes these panics inevitable. This latter group of economists has grown to such an extent that when the late Irving Fisher took a poll of the members of the American Economic Association in 1947 to determine how many of them favored reform of our banking system so as to remove the basic cause of bank panics, over 1,100 of them signified their approval—many of them well-known economists and heads of their departments at their respective universities.

Main Cause for Bank Panics

It is difficult to understand why anybody should be in doubt as to the main cause of bank panics. When men engage in a "run on a bank," they do it for a very obvious reason. They are afraid their money isn't there. They're afraid that if they don't withdraw the money they have a right to withdraw, they may lose it altogether. And their fear is perfectly justified under a system of fractional reserve banking. Their money is *not* there—nor is it anywhere. Only a small fraction of their money has an actual physical existence. All the rest of it is nothing but *book entries* against which the depositors can draw checks.

"How do the book entries come into existence?" you ask.

Our banks have the privilege of *creating* such book entries and lending them to the public so long as they maintain a certain minimum cash reserve. Hence, the name "fractional reserve banking." And in proportion as banks exercise this privilege of creating deposits and lending them, and as checks are drawn against these imaginary deposits and used to pay for goods and services and then deposited in other banks, the total amount of imaginary deposits grows. This means our banks become less and less liquid, i.e., less able to pay their depositors in cash if called upon to do so on a large scale. The more illiquid the banking system becomes—the more inevitable it is that a loss of confidence will occur. When it finally occurs it takes either the form of a financial panic, or a contraction in business resulting from fear that a panic or "credit crisis" may occur, or a combination of both as in the period 1929-33.

The fact that the National Bank Holiday didn't occur until 1933 has led many people to believe that the Great Depression which was heralded by the stock market crash in 1929 was not caused by the banking system. But as early as 1928 the financial advisers of some of our large corporations were getting increasingly uneasy about the weak condition of our banks. Faced with the likelihood of another financial crisis, the only sensible thing for them to do was to advise the curtailment of capital expenditures, a liquidation of inventories, and a reduction of indebtedness to the banking system. These very actions, of course, hastened the thing that was feared. But the fears were certainly justified—as later events proved: 1,352 banks suspended payments in 1930, and 2,294 suspended payments in 1931. Many of those who hadn't foreseen this financial trouble or who were lulled to sleep by Hoover's repeated assertions that the Federal Reserve System was panic proof, lost their businesses.

An economist for one of our largest banks, when confronted with the foregoing explanation of what it is that causes a loss of confidence at the height of each boom, attempted to disprove this theory with the following argument: The fact that our large corporations did not withdraw their bank deposits when they first began liquidating and curtailing operations is clear evidence they did not fear a collapse of the banking system. Had they feared such a collapse, he reasoned, the first thing they would have done is withdraw their deposits.

The answer to this is that for every dollar of bank deposits held by these corporations, there were hundreds of dollars in inventories that had to be liquidated. Their primary concern, therefore, was to liquidate their inventories before trouble with the banks developed. If they were so rash as to withdraw their bank deposits when they first anticipated trouble with the banks, they would have taken great losses because of their inability to liquidate large inventories produced at an inflated price and wage level.

Are Things Different Today?

Defenders of this unsound system of banking hasten to assure us today that things are different. They claim that the banking reforms made since 1933 have removed the possibility of another collapse such as we had in 1933. They point in particular to the Federal Deposit Insurance Corporation as a safeguard against wholesale bank failure. What they overlook, of course, is the fact that the basic weakness in our banking system still exists. We still operate on the assumption that the process of creating imaginary deposits is sound. The F.D.I.C. is nothing but a gimmick designed to bolster our confidence and trust in an untrustworthy system.

...

The time has come for us to face the fact that there is no such thing as a sound method of insuring deposits in a banking system that operates on unsound principles. *The creation and lending of fictitious deposits is not a sound method of banking.*

...

I believe that banking institutions are more dangerous to our liberties than standing armies. Already they have raised up a money aristocracy that has set the Government at defiance. The issuing power should be taken from the banks and restored to the Government to whom it properly belongs.

—Thomas Jefferson to John Taylor

Arguments Are Fallacious For World Central Bank

By Robert de Fremery
(Excerpts from the article published in *The COMMERICAL and FINANCIAL CHRONICLE*,
September 26, 1963)

...

Elgin Groseclose, financial consultant and Director of the Institute for International Monetary Research, has spotlighted the true nature of credit banking: "The practice of the goldsmiths, of using deposited funds to their own interest and profit, was essentially unsound, if not actually dishonest and fraudulent. A warehouseman, taking goods deposited with him and devoting them to his own profit, either by use or by loan to another, is guilty of a tort, a conversion of goods for which he is liable in civil, if not in criminal, law. By a casuistry which is now elevated into an economic principle, but which has no defenders outside the realm of banking, a warehouseman who deals in money is subject to a diviner law: the banker is free to use for his private interest and profit the money left in trust. ... He may even go further. He may create fictitious deposits on his books, which shall rank equally and ratably with actual deposits in any division of assets in case of liquidation." (*Money: the Human Conflict*, pp. 178-179.)

Disputes Concept of Surplus Reserves

One of the main arguments used by those who defend this unsound banking system is based on a misuse of the word "surplus." The argument is best understood in the context of those who first employed it. The early goldsmith banker noticed that when he operated honestly—with 100% reserves behind all outstanding notes and checking accounts—only a small fraction of the coin entrusted to him was ever withdrawn at one time. He therefore called the remainder "surplus" and determined to lend it out at interest. Actually, however, these "surplus reserves" were not surplus. The coin was idle in a physical sense only. Its ownership was changing constantly while titles to the coin (notes and drafts) were used as a medium of exchange. But the goldsmith-banker naively argued that the coin was not used because it still lay in his vault. With this specious excuse, the goldsmiths called their reserves "idle" or "surplus" and decided to use them for their own purposes.

There is still another way in which the "idle" or "surplus" reserves of these early goldsmiths were really very much in use. The goldsmiths had to have 100% reserves behind their notes and checking accounts in order to maintain the complete and lasting confidence of the public. Panic threatened whenever the public lost confidence in the ability of the goldsmiths to pay their depositors in full. Indeed, panics have shown the weakness of the system ever since it started. Goldsmiths who engaged in credit banking by issuing notes not backed by coin, or by creating imaginary deposits, did so on the assumption that they could eat their cake and have it too. They hoped to inflate the amount of paper money beyond the amount of coin they held, and still maintain the same confidence. Their inability to do so has been demonstrated repeatedly ever since the practice began. Logic was against the system from the start and all our experience has confirmed that logic.

H. L. McCracken gives another defense of the system: "In short, banks are no longer pure depositories, but rather 'Insurance Companies,' and as such they insure customers against all reasonable probabilities, but not the worst possibilities. It is conceivable that all should die of some epidemic in one year, or that a conflagration should wipe out cities by the score, but insurance rates are not pushed to the point sufficient to cover such contingencies. So in banking, it is practically possible that a banker may be called upon to pay all his liabilities in the form of deposits in a single day, which has been literally true in periods of fear, as revealed by 'runs' on the banks. But just as insurance companies do not anticipate pestilence and wholesale conflagration, so do bankers not anticipate wholesale financial calamity." (*Value Theory & Business Cycles*, p. 62-63.)

Insurance Companies Differ From Banks

The flaw in this argument is not hard to find. An insurance company, by insuring lives or property, does not *cause* a "pestilence and wholesale conflagration," whereas a banking system which is permitted to create and lend fictitious deposits—thereby placing itself in the untenable position of promising to pay on demand more money than is in their vaults—is actually responsible for the loss of confidence that eventually results in "wholesale financial calamity."

Orthodox banking theorists have traditionally slighted

the *confidence* factor. Long treatises have tried to prove the soundness of the credit banking system, but time and again, *lack of confidence* causes it to collapse.

Why do banking theorists persist in telling us that the system is sound, that confidence should not be lost, that depositors should not fear for the safety of their funds?

They argue: Even though a banker's cash reserves do not equal his total deposits, he has outstanding loans which, when repaid, can be used to pay the depositors in full. These outstanding loans may be secured by mortgages or other collateral. If for any reason the loans are not repaid, the banker can foreclose, sell the property, and pay the depositors with the proceeds. So why should a depositor ever lose confidence?

However, experience early showed the banking system could not liquidate in this way. Hence the entry in Samuel Pepys' Diary for Sept. 12, 1664, showing his distrust of England's first goldsmith bankers "because of their mortality."

Why does the banking system have trouble liquidating when confidence is lost? A general withdrawal of cash reserves causes the bankers to curtail further loans so as to decrease the outstanding claims against their meager reserves. This contraction of the medium of exchange causes the price structure to collapse, making it impossible for banks to collect their outstanding loans. And even though the banks foreclose, they cannot sell the foreclosed property for what it was originally worth. The same deflation which makes the repayment of all the bank loans impossible also shrinks the dollar value of the foreclosed property. ...

No Protection from Monetary Management

Many banking theorists contend that collapses of bank credit are not inherent in the system but rather result from "unwise" or "unsound" extensions of bank credit. But the validity of the foregoing arguments against the use of bank credit as money depends in no way upon the quality of bank credit. There is no wise or sound way of short-selling or debasing the legal standard of value. There is no wise or sound way for a banker to create imaginary deposits on his books against which checks can be drawn. There is no wise or sound way to indulge in an activity that is basically fraudulent and dishonest.

...

Two Principles

Two significant principles emerge.

1. The medium of exchange must coincide with the legal standard of value to have prices in terms of our legal standard. *This rules out credit banking.*
2. The value of a dollar depends upon the number of dollars in use rather than their mineral composition. This is merely an application of the law of supply and demand to money.

As Alexander Del Mar held: "Price implies precision. It is, or is intended to be a precise expression of value; and it approaches actual precision in proportion as the whole number is limited and known of the pricing symbols or denominators; because the whole number of such symbols is the only steady, stable, permanent immovable point from which such precise measure of value can be made." (*The Science of Money*, p. 20.)

... "The more exact the limits of the volume of money are defined in the law of each State the more equitable will it become in its operation upon prices and the dealings between man and man." (*Ibid.*, p. 129.)

There is good reason to believe many of our founding fathers did not intend to have the English system of credit banking imposed upon the newly formed United States. Under the Constitution each State gave up its right to issue bills of credit and Congress alone was given the power "to coin money and regulate the value thereof." Yet it wasn't long before banks were doing what in effect the states were forbidden to do. And we know that Madison, Jefferson and Clay all questioned the constitutionality of the United States Bank.

...

C. W. Barron obviously knew what was happening when the Federal Reserve Act was passed: "The purpose of the act most largely in its inception was 'for other purposes,' and these 'purposes' can never be wisely or effectively carried out; if persisted in they spell disaster to the country. The hidden purpose or 'motif' which inaugurated this legislation, however in effect it may work out under wise administration, is to cheapen money." (Requoted from Groseclose, *op. cit.*, p. 223.)

The disaster predicted by Barron hit us in the early 30's. The Federal Reserve System had made it possible to inflate the credit balloon further than ever before. When confidence finally cracked we had the worst deflation in history.

Commenting on this in 1934, Groseclose wrote: "As we survey the monetary situations in this country we discover that the distortions and convulsions which developed were the result of a people relying increasingly upon money to facilitate its commercial exchanges, while at the same time progressively weakening and deteriorating its money system. We had built a vast and splendid structure of technical economy, of organized commerce and integrated industry, upon the foundation of money, and while we were building this structure we were undermining the foundation by the device of deposit credit. We saddled upon money the burden of our entire economic functioning, the complicated and extensive machinery for the creation and distribution of goods, and then progressively weakened our money until it was no longer able to support the weight. In the years preceding the great stock market collapse of 1929 we had been going through a progressive inflation of the money, comparable in character, if not in degree, to that which occurred in Europe after the World War.

"Under the conditions that grew up around a situation of constantly expanding banking operations based on steadily diminishing reserves it was inevitable that a crash should occur. ... The stupendous house of banking had been built upon sand—public confidence in the infallibility and capacity of the institution—and when the sand began to shift, the whole structure toppled like an Egyptian monolith." (*Money, The Human Conflict*, pp. 241-245.)

Still not willing to come to grips with the basic problem, we patched the system again. The Federal Deposit Insurance Corporation was created. But obviously there is no safe way to insure deposits when banks retain the power to create them. The managers of the FDIC are well aware of its limitations. Their annual report for 1957 frankly said: "There is no question that the present deposit insurance would be entirely inadequate should, for example, a situation similar to that of 1930-33 recur." (p.65) More recently, Sam Fleming, then President of the American Bankers Association, recalled the rediscounting liquidity problem in the 1930's, said it could happen again, and suggested a more flexible administration of the discount window so as to solve once and for all the problem of a possible shortage of bank assets. (*Commercial & Financial Chronicle*, Jan. 22, 1962.)

Criticizes International Bank Moves to Inflate

If we squarely face the basic weakness of our financial system we will see how short-sighted we are to place our trust in the International Monetary Fund and any attempt to increase its lending power. What the world now needs is not some new international props to buoy confidence in a fundamentally unsound system. That will only open the way to further weakening of the credit structure. That is but adding weak links to a weak credit chain. What we need is basic reform of each country's monetary system so that each has a sound, noncollapsible monetary unit.

The creation of money must be divorced from the lending of money. The power to create money must be confined to governments alone *and limited by constitutional safeguards.* Banks must not be allowed to lend their credit, but only money placed with them for that purpose and therefore not subject to withdrawal while out on loan. Then and only then will all investments come from actual savings as they should.

The existing volume of bank credit, which is being used as money, will have to be monetized and completely divorced from gold. Some agreement must be reached concerning how to adjust the supply of money to population growth. This should not be difficult. ...

International equilibrium would henceforth be maintained by flexible exchange rates just as national equilibrium can be maintained by flexible prices.

...

Quotes Von Mises

A few years ago one of the world's truly great economists, Ludwig Von Mises, pin-pointed the principal cause of our economic ills as follows: "Yet most of the supporters of sound money do not want to go beyond the elimination of inflation for fiscal purposes. They want to prevent any kind of government borrowing from banks issuing banknotes or crediting the borrower on an account subject to cheque. But they do not want to prevent in the same way credit expansion for the sake of lending to business. The reform they have in mind is by and large bringing back the state of affairs prevailing before the inflations of the First World War. ... They still cling to the schemes whose application brought about the collapse of the European banking systems and currencies and discredited the market economy by generating the almost regular recurrence of periods of economic depression." (*The Theory of Money and Credit*, new edition, p. 439.)

Von Mises points to the real tragedy of our times—the "discrediting of the market economy." This means the shattering of man's faith in freedom. More and more men have lost faith in the ability of a free market to regulate itself. The true liberalism that flowered in the latter part of the

71

18th and early part of the 19th century has yielded to the determined onslaught of humanitarians bent on using the powers of government to alleviate the suffering and injustice they thought was caused by the operation of free market forces. Instead of eradicating the basic weakness in our banking system so as to make it possible for free markets to function properly, we allowed that weakness to continue and questioned instead the ability of free markets to regulate themselves. The western world has been steadily deteriorating ever since. Philosophies detrimental to the survival of freedom have been flourishing *and will continue to flourish* until such time as we are willing to mount a determined counter-attack by putting our financial system on a sound basis. It won't be easy to make the changes that have to be made. But there are no short-cuts to the survival of freedom. And although the task ahead of us is a difficult one, at least it holds the promise of solving the crisis of our times by going to the root of the trouble.

It (banking) is the most important subject intelligent persons can investigate and reflect upon. It is so important that our present civilization may collapse UNLESS IT IS WIDELY UNDERSTOOD AND THE DEFECT REMEDIED VERY SOON.

—Robert H. Hemphill,
former Credit Manager,
Federal Reserve Bank of Atlanta, Ga.

WHAT TO DO ABOUT THE DOLLAR

By Robert de Fremery
(Excerpts from the article published in *The*
COMMERCIAL and FINANCIAL CHRONICLE,
September 23, 1965)

On June 1, 1965, Wm. McChesney Martin* jolted the
financial world by pointing to "disturbing similarities between our present prosperity and the fabulous '20s."*But he*
didn't go far enough. He didn't pinpoint the underlying cause
of the disaster of 1929-1933. And obviously we can't avoid
another severe depression if we don't understand—or refuse to admit—the cause of preceding depressions.

The worst possible mistake we can make is to assume—
as Mr. Martin and many others do—that we can avoid
another collapse without making institutional changes. We
can't. Cycles of inflation and deflation are inherent in our
system of fractional reserve banking. The very basis of this
system is the unsound and unprincipled practice of borrowing short to lend long.

Bankers "borrow" the money you deposit in checking
accounts withdrawable on demand and lend it for as long
as 90 days and even six months. They borrow the money

---

* Chairman of the Federal Reserve Board at that time.

75

you put into savings accounts withdrawable on 30 days' notice and lend it for as long as 20 years.

The money thus loaned by banks is immediately deposited or credited to the account of the borrower—thus resulting in an expansion of bank deposits. As checks are drawn against these new deposits to pay for goods and services and redeposited in a checking or savings account with the same or another banker, the receiving banker repeats the process. He borrows short and lends long—increasing deposits still further.

Fraudulent Deposits

This essentially fraudulent practice multiplies bank deposits that exist only as book entries. Bankers become obligated to pay out on demand, or on 30 days' notice, money that doesn't exist. They place themselves in substantially the same position as a de Angelis or a Sol Estes. Both authorized the creation of titles to nonexistent goods.

The only difference is that we have legalized the banker's operation. But making this unsound practice legal doesn't prevent the public from periodically losing confidence and asking for its money. The result is panic and depression. Neither a banker nor a de Angelis can perform the magic of delivering something that doesn't exist.

When a panic occurs because of a suspected shortage of actual money, the small amount that does exist is naturally hoarded. Gresham's Law!

Debtors then go through the wringer. Bankruptcies multiply. Foreclosures rise. Prices fall. Unemployment mounts.

The cause-and-effect relationship between bank panics

and depressions was obvious in the early days of the system. But as the wiser members of the business and financial world finally learned the inevitable consequences of steadily increasing the amount of bank deposits that had no existence except as book entries, they began anticipating these panics by curtailing capital expenditures, reducing inventories, and getting out of the stock market.

These very actions, of course, serve as storm warnings to others. They in turn take protective measures that become storm warnings to still others. Finally a general loss of confidence occurs as a wholesale liquidation of stocks takes place in anticipation of a depression.

Many hold that if the banking system were based on an essentially fraudulent practice, it would have died a natural death long ago. Yes, that's what would have happened if the bankruptcy laws that apply to most businesses were applied to banks. But they aren't. When panics occur, the bankers (who have borrowed short from their depositors) are favored as compared with those who borrowed from the bankers.

Those who can't pay the banks are declared to be insolvent and forced into bankruptcy. But the banker who cannot pay his depositors on demand is not forced into bankruptcy. He is merely "technically insolvent." He is given the opportunity to foreclose on those who can't make their payments to him. Those who are really responsible for the panic—the bankers who borrowed short to lend long—can foreclose on others in an effort to obtain the money they (bankers) owe their depositors! The frightful injustice of this should be obvious.

...

International Extension

After the second world war, the world's central bankers decided to do what the United States did when it formed the Federal Reserve System. They decided to pool some of their reserves. The International Monetary Fund was formed to help any central bank in difficulty with the rest of the world. But after massive aid was given to Britain during the Suez crisis, members of the IMF realized the pool of reserves wasn't big enough, so they each put in still more. Even this was later felt to be inadequate, so the Paris Club was formed—a group of ten countries that agreed on a plan whereby the IMF could borrow from one or more of them in an emergency.

Soon the United States was making swap agreements with central banks of other countries (you come to my aid in a pinch and I'll come to your aid in a pinch). And the latest development is another proposed increase of each member's quota in the IMF—yet to be ratified by the legislative bodies of each member country.

Despite these frantic efforts to shore up this tottering edifice, a worldwide "confidence crisis" becomes more and more likely. Every central banker and all large financial interests know this. That is why various proposals to reform the international monetary system are being made today. But not one of the plans being discussed would solve the problem.

...

When will we come to our senses?

Stubborn adherence to an essentially unsound monetary system has been forcing us to adopt many unsound measures such as deficit financing, the Full Employment

Act, price supports, etc. The further we depart from sound economic principles, the more trouble we get into. This leads to demands for still more government controls.

Public Education

Our high schools and colleges are turning out graduates who have no faith in the operation of free market forces. Their teachers believe the so-called "business cycle" is inherent in a free enterprise system. It is not. Free markets cannot be expected to function smoothly without a sound and reliable money in terms of which prices can be expressed. Indeed it is a tribute to the inherent strength of a free enterprise system that it has survived as long as it has.

...

Once we admit the unsoundness of borrowing short to lend long, we will see the wisdom of converting our banks into lending institutions that borrow long to lend short. Government alone would then exercise its constitutional prerogative "to coin money and regulate the value thereof." And once government performs its legitimate function of providing our country with an adequate supply of money, banks could perform their proper function of safeguarding that money, facilitating the exchange of titles to money by means of checking accounts, and lending the savings of the community by borrowing long to lend short.

...

During the thirties there was widespread interest in the idea of 100% reserve banking. ... But because it was not considered "politically feasible," interest waned.

For over 200 years we have been doing what is politically feasible rather than what is economically sound.

That's why the world is in such a mess. And we can expect things to get worse if we continue letting expediency determine our actions.

...

My choice of a ghost, which could turn out to be a flesh-and-blood menace to our credit structure ... is the business of borrowing short and lending long.

—George W. Mitchell, Member, Board of
Governors, Federal Reserve System,
10/22/65

They (banks) must, after all, pay off most depositors on demand; in effect they, borrow funds for short, indeterminate periods. And to borrow short to lend long has never been a slogan of safe finance.

—Wall Street Journal editorial,
May 29, 1967

Most of England's balance of payments troubles are due to too much borrowing short and lending long ... the classic road to bankruptcy.

—James Callaghan, Chancellor
of the Exchequer, England, 1965

PERIODIC LIQUIDITY CRISES: THE REAL CAUSE AND CURE

By Robert de Fremery
(Excerpts from the article published in *The
COMMERCIAL and FINANCIAL CHRONICLE*,
October 20, 1966)

...

The last international liquidity crisis contributed heavily
to the rise of Welfare States, Naziism and World War II.
What will be the aftermath of the current crisis that is
worsening by the day? Does our government have the
courage to explain publicly the real cause of these recurring
crises?

There are glimmerings of hope. George Mitchell of the
Federal Reserve Board recently expressed concern about
the liquidity problems that have arisen from "the growing
business of borrowing short and lending long—the trans-
formation of liquid claims into longterm credits by depository intermediaries ... financial intermediaries have
implicitly promised more liquidity, yield and accommoda-
tion to their customers than they can readily deliver."*

However, Mitchell offers no constructive plan to avert

---

* Statement before Committee on Banking and Currency, May 24,
1966

the crisis. Instead he says: "In the short run, we have to quell the hysteria and break the paralysis that seems to be gripping some participants in and observers of the financial scene. The financial structure is essentially resilient and well managed, and there exist governmental mechanisms established for the very purpose of easing adjustments that must come in the wake of shifts in demands for goods and for financial services ... the situation hardly warrants the crisis atmosphere that has developed in some quarters, or the overreaction by portfolio managers which threatens to curtail housing activity unnecessarily sharply."*

Creating a Better System

Soothing words about the effectiveness of "governmental mechanisms" to deal with a liquidity crisis will not allay the fears of those who know its cause. There is only one thing that will allay those fears and that is to put our depository intermediaries on a sound basis. To do this we must convert the existing volume of bank credit into actual money and require banks to stop the unsound practice of borrowing short to lend long. ...

Under this stabilized system banks would have two sections: a deposit or checking-account section and a savings-and-loan section. The deposit section would merely be a warehouse for money. All demand deposits would be backed dollar for dollar by actual currency in the vaults of the bank. The savings-and-loan section would sell Certificates of Deposit (CDs) of varying maturities—from 30 days to 20 years—to obtain funds that could be safely loaned for

---

*   Statement before Committee on Banking and Currency, May 24, 1966

comparable periods of time. Thus money obtained by the sale of 30-day, one-year and five-year CDs, etc., could be loaned for 30 days, one year and five years respectively— not longer. Banks would then be fully liquid at all times and never again need fear a liquidity crisis.

...

Some believe it is too late to make such a radical change in our banking system. They forget the present system is so unsatisfactory that far more drastic plans for international monetary reform are being considered right now. The tragedy is that none of the other proposed plans comes to grips with the basic cause of our troubles. They all assume the soundness of borrowing short to lend long. They all involve a further loss of each country's financial sovereignty. Some want this and have been working toward this end ever since the last international liquidity crisis in the early 1930's. They sincerely believe liquidity crises can be averted by closer cooperation of all central banks. This is the same unsound thinking that originally led to the formation of all central banks. It is the thinking that led to the creation of our so-called "panic-proof" Federal Reserve System that gave us more inflation and deflation than ever before.

...

The United States is at an important turning point in its history. Until now we have been following the advice of those who persist in defending the practice of borrowing short to lend long. Are we going to continue—or are we going to admit that we have been led astray? Shall we give up our financial sovereignty, or shall we at long last provide ourselves with a reliable dollar? Time will tell. But of one thing we can be certain: A banking system based on the unsound practice of borrowing short to lend long is destined for oblivion. The sooner it goes—the better for mankind.

Borrowing short and lending long has been one of the classical recipes for vulnerability.
                        —Harold Wilson, Prime Minister of
                                        England, 4/14/65

The inconsistency of borrowing short and lending long has constituted a basic weakness in the banking system and has subjected long-term assets to violent deflation when banks have had to sell these assets rapidly to meet the demands of time depositors.
                        —W. Randolph Burgess,
          The Reserve Banks and the Money Market

As the world's banker, the U.S. now is indulging in a practice which most bankers consider ruinous: borrowing short, while lending long.
          —Barrons, "The World at Work", 9/12/60

SHOULD BANKS BE PERMITTED
TO BORROW SHORT AND LEND LONG?

(Published in the *The COMMERCIAL and FINANCIAL CHRONICLE*, July 20, 1967)

Yes! Says Dr. Walter Salant, Senior Staff Economist,
The Brookings Institution, Washington, D. C.
No! Says Mr. Robert de Fremery, President, Onox, Inc.,
San Francisco, Calif.

Whether or not banks jeopardize their existence because of the prevailing practice of lending on a long-term basis funds borrowed short term is the subject of a debate between Brookings Institution's top economist, who defends banks' intermediation methods, and San Franciscan manufacturer and writer on monetary economics, who claims that the failure to match borrowing and lending maturities is as unnecessary as it is dangerous. The debate stems from an Oct. 20, 1966 article by Robert de Fremery in the CHRONICLE which was republished by THE BUSINESS DIGEST (published monthly at 681 Market Street, San Francisco, Calif.) and which, in turn, led to an exchange of views between Mr. de Fremery and Dr. Salant in the April and May 1967 issues of THE BUSINESS DIGEST. The debate is reprinted here with the kind permission of all parties concerned.

BY DR. SALANT

As I understand it, your basic thesis is that the practice of borrowing short and lending long inevitably leads to instability because it causes the public sooner or later to lose confidence in bank deposits and ask for currency, which the banks, being illiquid, cannot supply. That result you regard as inherent in this method of bank operation.

I agree that some members of the public will always be wanting to convert bank deposits into currency. But others will always be depositing currency. The question is whether the net demand for conversion of deposits into currencies is unstable because of the banking practice which you criticize. I see no reason to think that it is.

I agree that other economic forces (which you do not discuss and apparently do not regard as central) may lead to general increases in the demand for currency and that when such increases do occur, a fractional-reserve banking system is more vulnerable to collapse in the absence of intelligent central bank action than a hundred per cent reserve system would be. Apart from economic factors, other than the bank practice of borrowing short and lending long, I see no great problem.

Like Insurance Companies

The situation of banks seems to me akin to that of insurance companies. They invest the proceeds of premiums in long-term assets despite the possibility that the insured may die. The foundation of their safety is that the proportion of people dying is rather stable, therefore predictable. Admittedly, the proportion of bank depositors who wish to convert deposits into currency is less stable.

But it is essential to my view that any tendency for this instability to reach crisis proportions arises primarily from factors originating outside the structure of the banking system itself, although these factors are reflected in expansion and contraction of bank deposits.

(I recognize that the analogy with insurance companies breaks down insofar as expansion of bank deposits increases the danger of bank failure and therefore the withdrawals, whereas expansion of insurance does not increase the proportion of insured people who die. My response is that deposit expansion itself does not increase the relative demand for currency much, if at all.)

If general economic policy is properly conducted, the loss of confidence to which you refer is not, in my view, inevitable.

Positive Argument

Now for the positive argument in favor of borrowing short and lending long. It rests on the importance of the economic function performed by financial intermediaries. This is more than a brokerage function. The argument for it has been developed only in the past six or seven years. (I have in mind the work of Messrs. Gurley and Shaw; e.g., their book *Money in a Theory of Finance*, published by the Brookings Institution in 1960.) ...

The essential point is that even though the amount of current saving and the amount of capital expenditures that other people wish to undertake in the same period may be equal, the assets which the savers wish to acquire may not be of the same kind that those who wish to make capital expenditures want to issue.

Savers, for example, may want highly liquid assets whereas would-be borrowers may want to issue only less liquid obligations.

Banks and other financial institutions supply liquid assets to the savers and take the less liquid securities of the would-be borrowers ... Performance of this function makes possible and also permits a given amount of saving to be transformed into investment with less use of economic resources.

You might agree that this should be done but say it should not be done by banks, whose liabilities are used as money. To this I can only ask why not? The stock of money is a portion of the total stock of financial assets and increases in it are one of the forms which current saving takes.

Central Bank Vital

If policy is so mismanaged as to permit large economic fluctuations of the kind that have led to widespread desire to convert deposits into currency, the remedy is to meet those crisis requirements through action by the central bank, the lender of last resort.

Since the Federal Reserve System has been in operation, we have had such a crisis only in 1932-33. That crisis would not have developed if the economic contraction had not advanced so far as it did.

I do think our understanding of economic policy is now good enough to make such an extreme situation no longer a major problem. But if it did arise, it could be handled through provision of reserves by the central bank.

Let me point out that immense shifts from deposits to currency now occur as a seasonal matter. They cause no trouble because central banks are quite prepared to deal with them by supplying reserves, regarding such operations as a routine technical matter. If avoidable crisis demands for currency are not actually avoided, they can be dealt with in the same way.

BY MR. DE FREMERY

Although we disagree as to the underlying cause of a general increase in the demand for currency, at least we agree a "fractional-reserve banking system is more vulnerable to collapse in the absence of intelligent central bank action." I would even question whether intelligent bank action could prevent a collapse. Time will tell.

But the important thing is: Why use a system that is vulnerable to collapse? I was puzzled by your defense based on an analogy with insurance companies. You say, "Deposit expansion does not increase the relative demand for currency much, if at all." Yet we have had panics periodically for the last 200 years. You reply by saying, "If general economic policy is properly conducted, the loss of confidence ... is not inevitable."

May I ask: What do you consider to be proper economic policy in the present situation in which all newly mined gold is going into private hoards because of the extent to which gold has been short-sold by the world's central bankers and their respective banking systems?

Vulnerability the Issue

I don't feel you answered any of the reasons I gave for believing a confidence crisis is inevitable under such a system. You say the practice of borrowing short to lend long gives us a "system more vulnerable to collapse." Doesn't the extent of the vulnerability depend upon the extent of deposit expansion?

Shouldn't we expect business and financial interests to become less and less confident in the strength of a banking system that is getting more and more vulnerable?

Shouldn't economists recognize that the public *does* react this way even though you may think it unintelligent for them to do so?

Money Is Still Money

In your positive argument in favor of borrowing short and lending long, you say, "The stock of money is a portion of the total stock of financial assets." True. But money is still money, and other financial assets are not money.

Money has a very important function to perform as a standard of value. The process of borrowing short to lend long upsets the stability of the standard of value. You partially recognize this when you concede the vulnerability of the system.

Fed Helpless In Crisis

Your faith in the ability of central bankers to deal with confidence crises doesn't inspire me. The Fed must still maintain a 25% gold reserve behind its notes. Although it can exceed these limits, it can do so only by paying a tax which would rise quite steeply if reserve deficiencies penetrated below 20%. This tax must be added to reserve Bank discount rates.

In other words, even if banks were able to rediscount

all their assets, the price would be prohibitive. Actually, banks can't rediscount all their assets. See George W. Mitchell's article in *The Commercial and Financial Chronicle*, December 30, 1965. He has suggested a change in the law to make this possible. But, as the law now stands, we definitely can have a loss of confidence merely from fear of another liquidity crisis.

The tragedy is that when another crisis occurs, persons with your faith will blame it again on "mismanagement." Even today the Federal Reserve Board is badly split on policy measures. Each individual thinks he can manage the monetary system—but they disagree among themselves as to what constitutes sound management. Wouldn't it be wise—in view of all the disagreement—to convert to a less vulnerable system that requires no "management" as such?

Sound Lending Needed

Real capital formation is desirable and is facilitated by financial intermediaries. But the practice of borrowing short to lend long is not a sound method of intermediation. You ask, "Why not?" Because it gives us what you admit is a vulnerable system. The likelihood of a loss of confidence increases the more vulnerable the system becomes.

As I see it, the only reason (and I do not consider it a valid reason) for allowing banks to borrow short to lend long is that it makes possible an expansion of "the supply of money." But that is not a proper function of the banking system.

I distinguish sharply between the government's legitimate function of providing our country with an adequate supply of money and the banks' legitimate function of acting as financial intermediaries. Because we have allowed banks to interfere with the government's function, the government has been forced to interfere with the banks in a multitude of ways.

I do not believe it possible for banks to resist an eventual government control of all banking unless they put their house in order by having what George S. Moore called "a back-to-back relation" between loans and CD's. George W. Mitchell calls it "meshing the maturity profile of assets and liabilities."

Well, so much for that. I am concerned about the future of our country. If my reasons for thinking the present system unsound are invalid, please tell me where I've gone astray.

REBUTTAL BY DR. SALANT

Let me try to identify basic points which may underlie the differences in our views.

One is that so long as the demand of asset-holders for liquid financial assets exceeds the amount of such assets which borrowers are willing to have outstanding as liabilities against themselves, and their demand for long-term assets is less than such borrowers want to issue at existing short and long-term interest rates, there are bound to be intermediaries which—in the absence of restrictions on arbitrage between the short and long-term markets—will create the short-term assets which the savers want, and purchase the longer-term liabilities which the borrowers want to issue.

The only way you could stop this would be to require

that the time pattern of intermediaries' liabilities and assets be the same. If this requirement were imposed, the rates of interest in long-term and short-term markets could differ greatly.

If the differential were great, incidentally, such regulation would be hard to enforce, but the main point is that such a barrier would inhibit some uses of current saving that are more socially desirable (as judged by the market) than some of the uses that would be promoted. Avoidance of this misallocation is the benefit that we get for the risk you regard as great and I regard as slight.

Restrict Banks Only?

Perhaps your response to this is that you have no desire to prevent all intermediaries from borrowing short and lending long; you merely want to stop banks from doing so, while allowing non-bank intermediaries to continue the practice.

If this is your answer, then I think the difference between us probably rests, at bottom, on your view that "money is still money, and other financial assets are not money." You apparently feel that, because of this distinction, what is permissible for non-banks should not be permitted for banks.

In my view, the distinction between money and non-money financial assets is not so sharp as your statement implies. It does not really matter very much whether the liabilities issued by those who lend long and borrow short are money or close substitutes for money. The "moneyness" of a financial asset is a matter of degree.

I realize that this view may be hard to accept; the belief

that the distinction between money-creation and inter-mediation is sharp dies hard, even among professional economists—it is in fact having a certain revival—but I think it is mistaken.

Fractional reserve banking is a response to the difference in the demand for long and short-term assets as between holders and issuers of financial assets. Any attempt to prevent the banks from bridging that difference would only result in its being bridged by some other existing or newly developed institutions.

Faith In Fed

You say we have had panics periodically for the last 200 years. As I pointed out in my earlier letter, we have had only one banking panic in the 50 years since we have had a lender of last resort, and that did not occur until a late stage of an economy-shattering depression.

You ask what I consider proper economic policy in the present situation in which all newly-mined gold is going into private hoards. That question introduces problems of international liquidity which I consider unrelated to fractional reserve banking in the domestic sphere. I think the present international monetary system has some serious defects but shall not go into them here; they are not related to domestic fractional reserve banking.

I certainly agree that the 25% gold reserve requirement behind Federal Reserve notes makes no sense. It immobilizes our gold holdings for the only purpose they can usefully serve. It should be abolished. Every competent economist I know is of the same opinion on this point. But the presence of this requirement is not an indictment of fractional reserve banking.

If it is a fact that business and financial interests really are becoming less and less confident in the strength of the banking system, I should agree that economists ought to recognize it. But I do not think that the banking system is becoming more and more vulnerable, and I do not think business and financial interests think it is.

Summarizes Position

My fundamental points are:

1. that borrowing short and lending long is a basic aspect of intermediation
2. that there is no special reason why banks should not be among the intermediaries performing this function, both because the distinction between their liabilities and those of other intermediaries is not a sharp one and because, with a lender of last resort, there is no reason, short of gross mismanagement to expect the difficulties you fear.

REBUTTAL BY MR. DE FREMERY

You are correct in saying: "The only way you could stop this (borrowing short to lend long) would be to require that the time pattern of intermediaries' liabilities and assets be the same." One Governor of the Federal Reserve Board calls this "meshing the maturity profile of assets and liabilities" (private correspondence). I asked this Governor if he favored banks doing this and he replied: "Every step in that direction has a stabilizing effect on the economy whenever the economy is confronted with real or fancied disturbances affecting people's desire for liquidity." (letter, 5-18-66)

There is no doubt this could cause rates of interest in long-term and short-term markets to differ greatly. But that would not make it difficult to enforce such a regulation.

Easy To Enforce

When the public fully understands that the practice of borrowing short to lend long causes a debasement of our standard of value, few persons will engage in such an action—either as borrowers, lenders, or intermediaries. It would be only the criminal element in society that would need to be watched—just as we watch for counterfeiters today.

Money Still Money

The holders of CDs issued by the now defunct San Francisco National Bank would certainly disagree with your belief "it does not really matter very much whether the liabilities issued by those who lend long and borrow short are money or close substitutes for money."

The public justifiably makes a sharp distinction between legal tender and bank deposits they may not be able to get the next day. Bank panics would not occur otherwise.

No Faith in Fed

My last letter explained why I could not share your faith in the ability of the Federal Reserve to prevent a severe confidence crisis. Your reply does not reassure me. You say the only banking panic we have had since the Fed's existence was due to "an economy-shattering depression." But

I gave reasons ... why that depression was brought on by the expectation of trouble with the banks. There was no reply to this.

Naturally the protective measures taken by those who saw the crisis coming started the economy downhill. But the blame should fall squarely on the weak banking system—not on those who were trying to protect themselves from that weak system.

You divorce problems of international liquidity from fractional reserve banking. Seems to me that one grew out of the other ... As pointed out by James Callaghan, Chancellor of the Exchequer: "Most of England's balance of payments troubles are due to too much borrowing short and lending long ... the classic road to bankruptcy."

Negotiable CDs Solve Problem

The "gap" between savers who want liquidity and borrowers who want funds for a stated period of time would cease to exist if we would simply give banks more freedom to use negotiable CDs of varying maturities to fit the needs of borrowers. Banks could then lend for stated periods of time without putting themselves in a vulnerable position; and savers would have their desired liquidity in the form of negotiable CDs. This is what George S. Moore, President, First National City Bank, sees so clearly (although he apparently does not wish to extend his line of reasoning to include all bank lending.)

Gold Hoarding Significant

You say, "There is no reason, short of gross mismanagement, to expect the difficulties you fear." But my point is that the system is so unsound it is impossible for central bankers to prevent a breakdown. That is why so much gold has been going into private hoards the last few years. You do not wish to relate these things. But sooner or later we're going to have to admit the cause and effect relationship between inflationary practices and the hoarding of gold.

Have you had a chance to read Stephen V. O. Clarke, *Central Bank Cooperation 1924-31*, recently published by the Federal Reserve Bank of New York? After reading it you may still feel that the system is manageable. But it had the opposite effect on me.

Summarizes Position

My fundamental points are:
1. the practice of borrowing short to lend long need not be a basic aspect of intermediation
2. the economy—both domestic and world—would be far more stable without that type of intermediation
3. that type of intermediation has such disastrous consequences on both domestic and world economic affairs that we are being forced to accept more and more government intervention in market processes—a distinct threat to our freedom.

BANKING REFORMS
TO STOP PERIODIC LIQUIDITY CRISES

By Robert de Fremery
(Excerpts from the article published in *The
COMMERCIAL and FINANCIAL CHRONICLE*,
July 9, 1970)

Milton Friedman has proposed two solutions to our money problems. Both have the same objective: to stabilize the rate of increase in the money supply. But in one case he would try to do this within the framework of the existing system of fractional reserve banking; in the other he would have us convert to a system of 100 per cent reserve banking.*

...

Quotes Letter from Friedman

Friedman says either remedy will work. If he is wrong, the consequences could be tragic. This whole matter deserves public debate. To further this, Friedman has given me permission to quote from a letter which, to my knowledge, is the most recent statement he has made on this subject: "I am as you say in favor of the 100 per cent reserve

---

*   *Essays in Positive Economics*, Milton Friedman, The University of Chicago Press, 1953, pp. 135-36.

scheme. I have been and I have written in favor of it in my *Program for Monetary Stability* and elsewhere. However, I do not attribute to this reform the importance that you attribute to it. I believe it would be a desirable reform but a relatively minor one. Without the 100 per cént reserve reform I believe it is possible to prevent depressions, liquidity crises, and the rest. Indeed as I said in a talk given in 1953, reprinted in my *Dollars and Deficits,* 'Why the American Economy is Depression Proof,' I believe that the legislation enacted in the 1930's, in particular the establishment of the FDIC, has made almost impossible a major liquidity crisis and monetary collapse of the kind we had in 1929-1933.

"I nonetheless favor the 100 per cent reserve plan for two reasons. The first is that under 100 per cent reserves it would be easier to get rid of government regulation of borrowing and lending. The second is that under 100 per cent reserves it would be easier and more mechanical for the Federal Reserve or a corresponding agency to control the behavior of the quantity of money. However, even without this reform there is no great technical difficulty in the Federal Reserve making the quantity of money behave in any way that it desires including a steady rate of increase in the quantity of money. The only problem raised by fractional reserves is that the authorities must offset changes in the reserve ratio and changes in the ratio of currency to deposits. Since in the absence of crises these tend to move very slowly there is no significant technical problem." (letter, January 21, 1969)

Banking's Fatal Error

First a word about how fractional reserve banks operate. Most people do not know that the bulk of our money supply is "privately created" by our commercial banks. The process is called "borrowing short and lending long.

. . .

The panic of 1907 led to demands for reform. But instead of facing up to the cause of the trouble we installed the so-called "panic-proof" Federal Reserve System (Fed). The idea was to pool the cash reserves of all banks and use this pool for massive loans to banks that needed more cash in a hurry. The Fed was also given the power to create more cash and lend it to member banks on the security of certain assets designated by law. We found—during 1929-33—that the system was still not panic proof.

Henry Simons' Proposal

After that debacle, the 100 per cent reserve proposal was made by Henry Simons in *A Positive Program for Laissez Faire*.* The purpose of this reform was to prohibit the practice of borrowing short and lending long—thus stopping the private creation of money by banks. As more money is needed in our country it would be the government's responsibility to provide it "under simple, definite rules laid down in legislation."** Our supply of money would henceforth be homogeneous. Gresham's Law would

---

*   This originally appeared in 1934. Now found in *Economic Policy for a Free Society*, Henry Simons, Univ. of Chicago Press, 1948, pp. 40-77.

**   Ibid, p. 57.

cease to bother us. *This reform would have gone to the root of the problem.*

...

We should heed the warning given by the Economic Policy Commission of the American Bankers Association in 1957: "Certainly, federal deposit insurance has greatly reduced the danger of widespread currency withdrawals. It should be recognized, however, that *the realization on the part of large depositors that their deposits are not fully covered might cause them in a time of uncertainty to shift some of their deposits.* In this connection, it may be noted that while the proportion of accounts fully protected by deposit insurance is about the same (98 per cent) for all size classes of banks, the proportion of dollar totals covered by insurance varies greatly, ranging from about 90 per cent in the smallest-size banks to roughly a third in the very large ones."* (emphasis added)

There were $194.8 billion of *uninsured* deposits in banks insured by the FDIC at the end of 1968. The possibility of a significant shift of some of these deposits could well be the *cause* rather than the *result* of some of the uncertainty existing in our financial markets.

Usually bankers, confronted with the facts about the FDIC and asked what would happen in the event of trouble, shrug their shoulders and reply that the government would simply print more money in a hurry to save the situation. But would it? Following the collapse of the stock market in 1929, President Hoover twice assured the American people that the Federal Reserve System had made our banks "panic

---

*   *Money, Financial Institutions, and the Economy,* A Book of Readings, Crutchfield, Henning, and Pigott, pp. 79-80.

proof." Yet, 5,099 banks suspended payment during the next three years.*

...

Jack M. Guttentag, Professor of Finance, Wharton School, in a recent address to the Investment Bankers Association, defined a financial panic as: "A general loss of faith in the capacity of those who have promised to provide cash under stipulated conditions to deliver on their promise—and a consequent rush by those to whom the promises have been made to convert them quickly, before others do so and before the resources of the promisor are exhausted."**

He added: "In days past the main promise at issue during financial panics was the promise of commercial banks to convert deposits into currency, but this is not at issue today."

Isn't it? What about the warning in his concluding note: "In addition, increasing attention will have to be paid to defensive open market operations. In this connection, the content of the directive given by the FOMC to the manager requires careful study. As I read the proviso clause that is now incorporated in the directive, *it could cause the manager to desert the market, even to withdraw reserves if there is an unexpected bulge in panic borrowing.*" (emphasis added)

As things now stand the promise of commercial banks to convert deposits into currency is still the main promise at issue today. Just because large depositors are not yet

---

*   Annual Reports of the Federal Reserve Board.

**   "The Federal Reserve in the Money Market", Jack M. Guttentag, *Commerical and Financial Chronicle*, May 7, 1970, p. 9.

asking for cash doesn't mean they now have confidence in the commercial bankers' promises to pay cash if called upon to do so. It is more plausible that they are not yet asking for cash because they know full well how shaky the whole structure is. Most large depositors are corporations that hope to continue doing business on a profitable basis. They also wish to maintain good banking relations. So when they first fear a liquidity crisis, they evidence that fear in ways other than withdrawing their money from the banks. They engage in anticipatory borrowing—thus causing interest rates to rise. These rising rates—like a falling barometer—have always heralded an approaching financial storm. *And no storm was ever prevented by tinkering with the barometer.*

Giant Squeeze Play

More needs to be said about the effects of this anticipatory borrowing. When a corporation or a utility floats a large bond issue, the net effect is a transfer of deposits from many small banks (from savings accounts of individuals attracted by the higher yields on bonds) to a large bank with whom the corporation or utility does business. Isn't it possible that some of the anticipatory borrowing actually may be encouraged by the large banks for this express purpose? In other words, a gigantic squeeze play could be going on between the large banks and the small banks for deposits. It isn't too difficult to see who would win that struggle. It would be tragic for many small banks. And the resulting failures could very readily trigger a general loss of confidence that would soon be felt by the larger banks that are even more vulnerable than the smaller ones.

Many frown upon such blunt talk. They say it may

precipitate the very panic that is feared. But we certainly cannot expect to make a rational improvement in the system without talking about the problem. *And a system that is so fragile it can't be talked about certainly needs improving.*

Discount Window

Friedman's proposal to have the Fed keep the supply of money expanding at a given rate per annum via open market operations would remove the possibility of a collapse of the supply of money. But banks would still be subject to runs because of their method of operation. And if the Fed's power to rediscount were abolished—as Friedman recommends*—the Fed would no longer be a "lender of last resort." *Wouldn't this tend to invite a panic?*

Presumably in the event of another panic, the Fed—under Friedman's prescription—would be pumping money into the country via open market operations at the same rate as dollars were being extinguished by bank failures. And, as Friedman pointed out in his letter, the authorities would have to offset changes in the reserve ratio and changes in the ratio of currency to deposits. This does not appear to be a very practical means of achieving monetary stability.

Would it help if the Fed kept its power to rediscount? Banks do not like to borrow from the Fed. It is a sign they have not conducted their affairs with prudence. It also frightens large depositors who know the Fed has first claim against a bank's assets in case of liquidation.

---

*   *Money, Financial Institutions, and the Economy*, Op. Cit., pp. 305-6.

Even if banks were willing to borrow on a large scale from the Fed, there is some question whether the Fed would oblige. J.L. Robertson, Vice-Chairman, Federal Reserve Board, in an address before the Ohio Bankers Association, said: "The discount window will, of course, always be there to protect communities and to meet the emergency needs of banks. But it would not be wise to count on its being there to save bankers from the consequences of going overboard in borrowing short and lending long."*

There is no doubt that banks have gone overboard. Let us face that fact and put our banks on a 100 per cent reserve basis now—thus making *certain* a banking crisis cannot occur.

Friedman said that one reason he would favor the 100 per cent reserve proposal is "it would be easier to get rid of government regulation of borrowing and lending." That is certainly a desirable goal. But the fact is there is not the remotest possibility of getting rid of such government regulation under a system of fractional reserve banking. Marriner Eccles, former Chairmen of the Federal Reserve Board, saw this clearly: "Credit must primarily be controlled at the source of its creation, the banking system. This cannot be done on a basis of voluntary agreements in a competitive business involving fifteen thousand banks. There must be adequate powers in the Federal Reserve System to bring about the needed restraint on the part of

---

* "Meeting Changing Banking Problems Before a Crisis," J. L. Robertson, *Commercial and Financial Chronicle*, Feb. 18, 1965, p. 12.

banks as well as on the part of borrowers."*

Eccles realizes that the supply of money is a Congressional responsibility that has been delegated to the Federal Reserve System. Therefore, if we use bank credit as money, the Federal Reserve System must have the power to control the banking system. But do we realize the extent of the controls that will be required? Says Louis B. Lundborg, Chairman of the Board, Bank of America: "The time has come to seriously consider expansion of Federal Reserve control. Control over only commercial banks is no longer sufficient for effective control of credit availability. The credit market in the United States is made up of much more than the commercial banking system."**

The essence of a free market economy is that men are free to work where they please and produce what they think is wanted by their fellow-men. Freedom to produce what you want requires a free banking system that mobilizes the voluntary savings of the community and makes these savings, available on a sound basis to the highest bidder. Centralized control of borrowing and lending means financial dictatorship. The Russians call it "control by the ruble."***

Do we want "control by the dollar?" We are headed in

---

* *Beckoning Frontiers*, Marriner S. Eccles, Alfred A. Knopf, 1951, p. 473.

** Address before the National Industrial Conference Board's National/International Financial Conference, Waldorf Astoria Hotel, Feb. 14, 1968.

*** See "Economic Control Through Credit Control", contained in *The Soviet Financial System*, Mikhail V. Condoide, Ohio State University, 1951, Bureau of Business Research, p. 38.

that direction. We are blaming our troubles wrongly on our free enterprise system instead of our unsound banking system. A dollar is a standard of value. A stable supply of dollars is therefore extremely important. Our society is as dependent on the accuracy of that standard as it is on the accuracy of our standards of length or weight. We foolishly allowed our banks to debase our dollars by the unsound practice of borrowing short and lending long. That led to so many economic ills that our whole economic system is now threatened.

Some say reform is not politically feasible. But can our republic survive without a reliable standard of value? Let's admit that when something is causing trouble, nothing is more impractical than to worry about the effects while ignoring the cause. Borrowing short and lending long— when combined with the clearing operations of a commercial banking system—makes our standard of value unreliable. It is therefore imperative that we:

1. put our banks on a sound basis now so they won't collapse again
2. insist that banks operate on a sounder basis in the future
3. pass a constitutional amendment that will keep our supply of money at whatever level is deemed necessary to support our economy.

This can be accomplished without depriving anyone of a single dollar he has access to today—and without adding to the supply of money. To whom should we look for leadership to bring about this much needed reform? To our bankers. They should see the handwriting on the wall more clearly than anybody. They know the problems that arise from borrowing short and lending long. They know the long arm of government will control them more and more if they persist in continuing this practice. And they know there is a sounder method of intermediation—the method suggested by George S. Moore, President, First National City Bank of New York. His bank first introduced the negotiable certificate of deposit (CD) in the early 1960's.

Misuse of CDs led to the credit crunch in 1966. Banks had been making five year loans with funds obtained by the sale of one year CDs. This led to a runoff of CDs when the return on good commercial paper exceeded the interest rate banks were permitted to pay. The resulting liquidity squeeze was so acute even during 1965 that there was some talk of restricting the issue of CDs. It was then that Moore proposed a more sensible solution: "It would reduce the risk of being illiquid if there could be a 'back-to-back' relationship between term loans and CDs—i.e., a five-year loan with a 5 ½ per cent yield would be based on a five-year CD paying a 4 ½ per cent interest rate. That way the banks could budget their income and obligations more precisely."*

This is refreshing rationality. Although Moore was referring only to CDs as currently being used, he stated a principle upon which all financial intermediation by banks should be based. All funds loaned by banks should come from the issue of negotiable CDs with maturities and yields tailored to meet the needs of borrowers and savers. And banks should be required to maintain a 'back-to-back' relation between loans and CDs. Banks would then have

---

*   *Fortune Magazine*, September, 1965, pp. 269-270.

100 percent cash reserves behind their checking accounts. There would be no savings accounts. Those with savings would buy negotiable CDs. Liquidity squeezes such as we have had in the past would then be an impossibility. There would be no more borrowing short and lending long— none of the multitude of problems and changing expectations caused by that unsound practice—and no excuse for any controls of borrowing and lending except to maintain the 'back-to-back' relation between loans and CDs.

When the above suggestions were brought to the attention of a member of the Federal Reserve Board, he replied: "I certainly have no quarrel with the commercial bank ... or any other financial intermediary that succeeds in *meshing the maturity profile of its assets and liabilities.* More power to it! Every step in that direction has a stabilizing effect on the economy whenever the economy is confronted with real or fancied disturbances affecting people's desire for liquidity." (letter, May 18, 1966. Emphasis added)

Any responsible citizen must mesh the maturity profile of his assets and liabilities. How else can he keep from going bankrupt? Shouldn't we expect an equally high standard of our bankers—those who are entrusted with the life savings of so many of our citizens?

The Panic of 1907 led to the Federal Reserve System— *which did not solve the problem.* The collapse of 1933 led to the FDIC—*which still has not solved the problem.* It is the responsibility of our bankers to spare us another such calamity. They can do it. Congress will pass the necessary legislation when our bankers ask for it. If that legislation is not passed before another calamity occurs, there is grave danger of our being swept into complete "control by the dollar" or, worse still, of losing our financial sovereignty. Will our bankers rise to the challenge?

In its principle, the reform of the credit mechanism should make impossible the exnihilo creation of money and the borrowing at short term to finance loans of a longer term, and it would permit only loans at maturity terms shorter than those corresponding to the funds borrowed.

—Maurice Allais, 1989 Nobel laureate
in economics in a paper delivered
that year in Montreal.

THE ONE HUNDRED PER CENT RESERVE PROPOSAL REVISITED

by Robert de Fremery
(Exerpts from a paper submitted to the Research
Department, Federal Reserve Bank of San Francisco,
November 6, 1976)

...

Now let's take a look at a possible method of converting to a 100% reserve system, a method that E.S. Shaw (Stanford), T. Mayer (U.C. Davis), and Martin Bronfenbrenner (Duke)*, have all said deserves serious consideration. None of them think such a reform is necessary at this time, but they agreed that it would be a good idea to have such a plan "in the offing" just in case the Fed proved unable to achieve the monetary stability our economy needs.

In what follows, I am purposely not going to use any actual figures. Figures aren't important at this time. It's the concepts that are important.

Since the objective is to have a 100% cash reserve (legal tender) behind all demand deposits, the U. S. Treasury would be ordered by Congress to have printed and then loaned to the banks sufficient new currency to fulfill that

---

* Each of these professors has been a visiting scholar at the Federal Reserve Bank of San Francisco.

objective. In determining the amount to be borrowed, banks would treat their legal reserves at their local Federal Reserve Bank as cash. Those reserves will become actual cash as explained later.

The debt incurred by each commercial bank to the Treasury could be immediately reduced by the amount of U.S. securities each bank held—simply a cancellation of mutual indebtedness. Henceforth the commercial banks would be prohibited from using the cash reserves behind their demand deposits for their own interest and profit. Those cash reserves belong to the depositors. They are funds against which the depositors wish to draw checks.

On the day the cash reserves of banks are brought up to 100% of their demand liabilities, they would have outstanding loans which I shall call "old loans"as distinguished from the new loans that will be made in the future. As these old loans are paid off, each bank would be required to use these funds to pay off their savings and time depositors, and offer them, as an alternative, negotiable CDs. There would be no restriction of any sort on the issuance of such CDs. The maturity dates, the amounts, and the rate of interest would be set by each bank. But banks would not be allowed to lend the funds so obtained for a longer period of time than those funds were available to them; i.e., they would be required to maintain the back-to-back relation suggested by George Moore.*

After each bank had paid off all its time depositors, it would still have a sizable amount of "old" loans outstanding. As the rest of these old loans were paid off, these funds

---

*   See page 113.

would be used to further reduce the banks' indebtedness to the Treasury. The Treasury, in turn, would be required to use these funds to retire U.S. obligations held by investors outside the banking system. And as the Treasury did this, these investors would presumably buy negotiable CDs offered by the banks.

Any remaining indebtedness of the banks to the Treasury could be paid off with funds derived from the sale of some of their "Other Securities". Indeed, a good argument can be made for having the Treasury figure in advance how much of each bank's securities are going to have to be sold and require them to start selling those securities gradually, the day the changeover is made.

As for the Federal Reserve Banks, they too should borrow from the Treasury sufficient new currency to bring their cash reserves up to 100% of their demand deposits (funds deposited by their member banks for safekeeping plus all government funds against which checks are being drawn by the government). The indebtedness of the Federal Reserve Banks to the Treasury could immediately be canceled by a mutual cancellation of indebtedness as was done by the commercial banks, i.e. by canceling an equivalent amount of U.S. obligations held by the Federal Reserve Banks. The remaining U.S. obligations held by the Federal Reserve Banks should also be canceled in view of the fact that they had originally been bought by the mere creation of bookkeeping entries. That practice would be abolished.

The supply of money would now consist of the total coin and currency in existence, i.e., the amount previously existing plus the amount newly printed and loaned to the commercial banks and the Federal Reserve Banks. There would no longer be any confusion about what was meant by the supply of money. And the money supply would no longer be altered by such things as the lending activities of banks, or the decisions of individuals to switch funds from a checking account to CDs, or the payment of taxes to the U.S. Treasury, or the disbursement of funds by the Treasury, etc. Whenever an increase in the money supply was needed according to whatever rule of law was adopted (a strong case can be made for a "population dollar", i.e., a constant per capita supply of dollars), the increase could be made with absolute precision by simply retiring that much of the remaining National Debt with the new money.

S & Ls and MSBs should be made to operate as they were originally intended, i.e., those who place their funds in such institutions must be reminded that they are shareholders and that they can draw their funds out only when those funds are available for withdrawal. A run on such institutions would no longer be a threat to the banking world. Nor would the failure or bankruptcy of any large bank, corporation, or municipality be the threat to the banking world that it is today. Any such poorly managed entity could, and should, be allowed to go through bankruptcy. There would be no danger of precipitating the type of financial stringency or credit crisis that is feared so much under our present financial system, and justifiably so.

The multitude of governmental lending agencies that have arisen since the early '30s should be dismantled. *The lending of money is not a proper function of government.* It has been sanctioned so far because banks operated in such a way as to imperil a continuous flow of funds to areas that needed it. With banks now operating on a sound basis, free market forces should be relied upon to keep money flowing in the most healthful manner for all.

Having corrected the destabilizing element of our monetary system, we should reject the concept of deficit financing and a compensatory budget. Those concepts arose under the old system because when the business and investment world lost confidence—thus leading to a contraction in the supply and/or velocity of money—the government was forced to indulge in deficit financing to try to keep the supply and/or velocity of money from contracting too far. Under the new system the supply of money is non-collapsible and therefore changes in the velocity of money (caused by changes in liquidity preference) would be minimal and self-regulating.

Government supervision or regulation of banks would now be greatly simplified. In place of all the governmental agencies with overlapping functions that are busily engaged in regulating various activities of banks, we need have only one agency. Its sole function would be to make certain each bank is keeping its cash reserves at 100% of its demand deposits, and that the maturity profile of its outstanding CDs meshes with the maturity profile of its loan portfolio. Except for these restrictions, banks would be free to set the amounts, the maturity dates, and the rates of interest on the CDs they issued. They would also be free to make loans for any purpose they pleased, secured by any collateral they deemed adequate.

. . .

Had a change like this been made in 1970, which is the last time I checked all the actual figures, the National Debt would have been reduced by over $200 billion. About half of that would have been instantaneous and the rest would still be in process today as the banks continue to retire the rest of their debt to the Treasury. Today, of course, those figures would be much greater.

What effect would all this have upon interest rates? It's hard to say. ... But the important point to keep in mind is that whatever happens to interest rates,—whether they rise, fall, or stay the same—it will be what should happen. Nobody can improve upon market forces for determining the proper rewards for working and saving *if* we have a sound money and tax system.

...

Some critics have questioned whether or not banks would be able to obtain sufficient long term lendable funds to meet the demand for such funds. No problem. Most savers will be buying long-term CDs in order to get a higher return because they know they will be able to sell their CDs in a secondary market should they need their funds before their CDs mature. Even today there are large amounts of long-term government securities currently held outside the banking system—securities that will be gradually paid off ahead of time as banks retire their debt to the Treasury. The amount of these is impressive: 1 to 5 years: $127 billion; 5 to 10 years: $35.6 b.; 10 to 20 years: $14 b.; over 20 years: $11.9 b. If many persons today are willing to lock up their savings in these securities whose ultimate real value at maturity is uncertain because nobody knows what will happen to the money supply in the meantime, will they not be even more likely to buy CDs of similar maturities when banks have been put on a sound basis, and the supply of money has been tied to our population by law?

However, let's suppose, for the sake of argument, that banks are unable to compete successfully for as much of the savings of the community as they have in the past. Suppose most savings flow directly into the commercial paper market or the municipal bond market or whatever. So what? Shouldn't market forces determine the use to which our savings are put?

I realize that many economists lack faith in market forces. But aren't they a little like the fellow who lost faith in his automobile because he persisted in using contaminated gasoline in the engine? Let's give free market forces a fair chance to show what they can do. And the first step in that direction is to provide ourselves with a sound and reliable money in terms of which economic decisions can be made.

CONCLUSION

Is it not obvious that there are serious defects in our banking system and our tax system that deprive most of us of fundamental rights and bestow enormous privileges on others? Could that not be the root cause of the problems that our country has today? Shouldn't we expect those problems to get worse if we fail to correct those defects?

Shouldn't all of us have equal rights, and none of us have special privileges? Shouldn't we take steps to secure our rights before the government plunges us into another war to divert our attention from our domestic problems?

I am only too well aware of the difficulties in making these reforms. One well known economist (who frankly admits these reforms should have been made long ago) says "It's too late now. You can't unscramble an omelet."

Can't we? Should we look upon ourselves as cracked eggs in a hot frying pan getting hotter by the day?

How many riots must we endure? How many prisons must we build? How many of our rights must we lose? How many of our young people must be sent away to fight in foreign wars before we decide that enough is enough?

It is for each of us to make a decision based on our own common sense. Jefferson had faith in our ability to govern ourselves if a free press kept us informed of the truth. I have that faith. I hope you do also. And each of us can help to spread the truth by sharing it with friends and neighbors.

A new public opinion must be created privately and unobtrusively. The existing one is maintained by the press, by propaganda, by organization, and by financial influences which are at its disposal. The unnatural way of spreading ideas must be opposed by the natural one, which goes from man to man and relies solely on the truth of the thoughts and the hearer's receptiveness for new truth ...

—Albert Schweitzer

Truth is violated by falsehood, but it is outraged by silence.

—Author Unknown

A pitiful wretch is he who knows the truth and yet can silent be.

—Author Unknown

Loyalty to petrified opinion never yet broke a chain or freed a human soul.

—Mark Twain

This is a world of compensation; and he who would be no slave must consent to have no slave. Those who deny freedom to others deserve it not for themselves, and, under a just God, cannot long retain it.

—Abraham Lincoln

Those who make peaceful change impossible make violent change inevitable.

—John F. Kennedy,

The punishment of wise men who refuse to take part in the affairs of government is to live under the government of unwise men.

—Plato

Until the protection of individual freedom is much more firmly secured than it is now, the creation of a world state would probably be a greater danger to the future of civilization than even war.

—Friedrick A. Hayek